William A. Martyr

3/6

OUR APPROACH TO GOD

OUR APPROACH TO GOD

A STUDY IN PUBLIC WORSHIP

BY

E. R. MICKLEM

CHAPLAIN, TUTOR AND LECTURER, MANSFIELD
COLLEGE, OXFORD
AUTHOR OF "MIRACLES AND THE NEW PSYCHOLOGY"

LONDON
HODDER & STOUGHTON, LIMITED

First printed 1934

PRINTED IN GREAT BRITAIN FOR HODDER AND STOUGHTON, LTD.,
BY RICHARD CLAY AND SONS, LTD., BUNGAY, SUFFOLK.

CONTENTS

CHAP.   PAGE

I.   INTRODUCTION 9

II.   WORSHIP, ITS NATURE AND ITS OBLIGATION 18

III.   THE CLAIM OF CORPORATE WORSHIP . 37

IV.   AN ARTIFICIAL ELEMENT NECESSARY IN THE CULT 51

V.   SACRIFICE 96

VI.   COMMUNION 112

VII.   PRAYER THE CHARACTERISTIC OF A WHOLE SERVICE . . . 142

VIII.   THE ARCHITECTURE OF A SERVICE. 212

IX.   THE LORD'S SUPPER . . . 244

Chapter
I
Introduction

' THERE is no surer sign of religious unrest ',
writes Archdeacon Lilley, 'than anxiety
about forms of worship.' * If that is true, then
religious unrest is widespread to-day. Whether
we judge by the books which are being issued
or by the many and various 'liturgical' movements which are to be observed in this country
and on the Continent, dissatisfaction with old-
established traditions in worship is evident
almost everywhere. In Great Britain gropings
after more effective ways in public worship can
be seen in nearly all denominations. While the
Church of England was engaged in promulgating
a revision of her Prayer Book the Nonconformists were presented with 'A Free Church Book
of Common Prayer'; and if Parliament openly
rejected the one and the Free Churches tacitly
rejected the other, that does not detract from
the significance of the events.

It is easy to point to numerous signs of dis-

* A. L. Lilley, *Worship, Its Necessity, Nature and Expression*, p. 30.

satisfaction in this country; it is no less easy
to point to similar signs at least as numerous in
the Protestantism of the Continent. We need
not stop to substantiate this statement—a long
chapter could be filled without difficulty in the
process. Suffice it to remind the reader of Dr.
Heiler's assertion that ' the liturgical problem
is one of the most important and most difficult
domestic problems of modern Protestantism '.*
And it is not in Protestantism only that questions of public worship are occupying men's
minds. Significant movements are discernible
in Roman Catholicism also. For example, we
may note on the one hand the tendency in some
quarters to lay preponderating emphasis on
subsidiary cults, such as that of the Sacré-
Coeur, and on the other the increasing efforts
to render intelligible to the faithful the
Liturgy in all its parts, a movement which has
its fount in the Benedictine monastery at
Solesmes.†

It is well to indicate this general state of
affairs summarily at the outset, because a
realization of it should enable us to see our
local and provincial problems in truer per-
spective and should arouse us to acquaint our-

* *Prayer*, E.T., p. 303.
 † On this latter movement vid. Heiler, *Katholischer und
Evangelischer Gottesdienst*, 2nd ed., p. 9 f.

selves with the activities of those in different lands and those belonging to widely differing ecclesiastical traditions who are giving thought and energy to the practical solution of the difficulties inherent in corporate worship.

But why, it may be asked, expend thought and energy at all on questions of worship? Has not the Church something better to do in these days of unemployment and economic stress, of social unrest, and of international rivalry? The Church has much else to do, certainly, but whether these other duties are 'better' or less good is a curious question, because in order that she shall accomplish anything the Church must live, and her life depends on her worship. If anyone is inclined to doubt this, let him consider what valuable contribution he thinks any Churches he knows have made and are making to life, and then let him try to think away all churches and chapels and Sunday services. How long does he suppose the Church's characteristic contribution would continue to be made once they had gone? A local church is a fellowship which may engage in a large variety of activities. Many of these activities—and they good ones—might cease, and yet it survive a living church; but let it cease its corporate worship, and its fate is sealed. This is inevitable, for its centre and focus is its worship. If it abandons that, it abandons its principle of cohesion and the very condition of its life as a church. What is true here of the local unit is necessarily true of denominations as a whole. Not even the Quakers would survive as a Christian body if they gave up their ' Meetings for Worship '.

It may be held that the churches have no useful function to perform in the modern world—that is another matter; but if anything is expected of them, then it is folly to blame them for concerning themselves with worship, because in so doing they are occupying themselves with that on which their continued existence depends.

This book is written with the life of the Free Churches chiefly in view, and it is expedient that its ecclesiastical standpoint should be made clear. While my interest is not sectarian (what is there lovely in denominationalism?), yet I believe that the Free Churches still have a contribution to give to the religious life of the country, and one which is for the benefit of that life. It is very desirable that we should have a better *ensemble* in our ecclesiastical orchestra, but it would be a mistake to accomplish this at the cost of abolishing the 'cellos or even the brass. The Church of England has been increasing her range in

more directions than one, but with all her
variety she does not yet possess a full com-
plement of instruments. Indeed, the sym-
pathetic observer has some reason to be uneasy
lest the increase of range should prove temporary. There are forces within the Anglican
communion which, should they triumph, would
mean the abandonment of orchestral work
altogether. This might spell a new acquisition
of power to Dissent, and it would certainly give
it a new opportunity; but no one, Nonconformist or Conformist, who cares for the Church
more than for Romanism, Anglicanism, or any
other -ism, could regard the event with any
satisfaction.

Canon F. R. Barry says: 'A religion is
rightly judged by its worship. People are right
in judging the Christian religion by what they
observe in our Christian Churches.' * I wonder
how the Christian religion comes off by the
test of Nonconformist worship to-day. Here
and there favourably enough, no doubt, but
usually and in most places? Let us Free
Churchmen ask ourselves a few questions, and
attempt to answer them frankly. What is the
condition of our mode of worship? Is it living, growing, and propagating itself? Do more
and more of those who are taking religion

* *The Relevance of Christianity*, p. 307.

seriously say, ' This is the worship for me, this
is the worship which expresses the faith I
would fain make my own '? It is a grave
conclusion if our answers have to be mainly,
No; but is there anyone who can honestly
affirm they should be, Yes? That chapels
were but scantily filled would not necessarily
prove a lack of vitality, for it may be that it
is the Church's part to be always only a rem-
nant in the world, but when those who would
be of the Christian fellowship turn their backs
on them the signs are ominous.

We need to go back to first principles. What
do we go to chapel to do? What is worship?
What constitutes an act of worship? What,
if anything, makes corporate worship obli-
gatory for the Christian? How should our
answers to these questions affect the content
and structure of a service? Have the Free
Churches any specific witness to make in this
matter? It is as a contribution to the answering of these and kindred questions that this
book is offered. They are not all easy questions,
and the discussion of some of them—and they
the most fundamental—may be found heavy
going, but I trust readers will not be put off
by this, because the questions are such as
Free Churchmen cannot afford to neglect to-day
if they believe that Nonconformity still has a

gift worth making to the life of Christ's Church.

Reference should be made to one feature of modern life which constitutes a danger to the Free Churches, though it is hardly inimical to religion : ' wireless ' and the broadcasting of services and sermons. Ecclesiastically speaking, in this country Rome alone has nothing to lose by the innovation. By no magic can the British Broadcasting Corporation enable you to bow in adoration before the elevated Host, and the most perfect auditory and visual (for that may come) representation of the Mass in progress can provide no sufficient substitute for presence at the mystery of transubstantiation and at the offering of the Sacrifice, or for actual participation in the oblation by what is called ' sacramental ' communion. The B.B.C. cannot help you to do better in your drawing-room what you might accomplish in an inferior way in your local Catholic chapel; but if what you want is a good sermon well delivered, and the ' uplift ' of a ' beautiful ' service, then it is many chances to one that your head-phones or loud-speaker can serve you better than your Dissenting conventicle or your Parish Church. The Dean of never-mind-what Cathedral, or Dr. you-know-whom-I-mean, has probably something far more interesting to say to you than has the occupant of any pulpit within a stroll from your house. Moreover, if, after you have ' switched on ', you find he does not suit your mood, there are no laws of courtesy to prevent your ' switching off ' again.

There are those in the Church of England who, in view of this state of affairs, think that the time is coming when the main use of the parish churches will be for the dispensing of the Sacraments. Whether or not that is a correct estimate may be doubtful, as also whether it is a prospect which Anglicans can regard with equanimity. Of the Free Churches, at all events, it is safe to say that they have no chance of survival if only those attend their chapels who come to ' take Communion '.

In theory, of course, the Nonconformist goes to chapel to join with the brethren in wor-shipping God, and in so far as that is his pre-vailing purpose, ' wireless ' cannot provide an adequate substitute for the chapel. Unfortu-nately (whether through his own fault we need not here decide) the chapel all too frequently provides neither the brethren in whose company he feels any strong desire to be nor the circum-stances of worship which would make cor-porate worship seem a valuable occupation; while, on the other hand, the chances are that the ' wireless ' Service will be at least edifying, and, oddly enough, 'listening in' may offer more satisfaction to the so-called 'herd' instinct than can be obtained by forming part of a scattered group in a relatively large building.

As I have indicated, it is my desire to make in this book a contribution helpful to the wise facing of what I believe to be a life-and-death issue for the Free Churches. To this end it is necessary to examine afresh the theoretical foundations of public worship, and hence I venture to hope that something may be found here of value also to others besides Nonconformists; but I have considered historical and philosophical presuppositions only in their bearing on the narrower issue named above, and it is none of my intention to undertake a task similar to that which Dr. Robert Will has performed in his monumental and invaluable treatise *Le Culte*. If, therefore, applications of principles and constructive suggestions are directed to a special 'cultural' tradition, it should be borne in mind that criticisms of existing practices have been likewise limited in their direction, and that they are not made for the delight of the scoffer, but for the honest scrutiny of men of goodwill who desire, not to break down, but to build up.

Chapter	Worship, Its Nature
II	and Its Obligation

I

WORSHIP implies the recognition of *worth*, and an act of worship is an expression of this recognition.

When a young man confesses to himself, or to his friend, that he 'simply worships' a certain girl, he means that he feels her to be *worthy* of all his devotion, and all the forms which his worship takes are so many expressions of his sense of *worth*.

For the Christian, religious worship is the ascription of absolute worth to God who evokes the sense of it. It is the response of the soul to God, who is, indeed, recognized as God because He is supremely worshipful.

In worship the centre of interest is the object which gives rise to it. Thus without a Godward orientation of the personality there can be no religious worship. That, perhaps, sounds a platitude. But is it? If it means that there must always be a Godward reference, possibly yes; but hardly if it means a concentration of interest on God—and the concentration of interest is a prerequisite of worship. If I entered a shop determined to buy a ready-made overcoat I should accomplish little without reference to the assistant, but there would be no necessity for me to have my interest centred upon him. Similarly, I may enter ' God's house ', or listen to ' God's spokesman ' by means of the wireless, in order to satisfy all manner of personal needs without ever being really turned Godwards in will and affection.

Worship means ' regard ', as indicating both the direction in which the personality of the worshipper is set, and the sense of ' worthfulness ' which the object of worship arouses. While granting this, many ask, What is the need for giving specific expression to this regard? Is not the regard by itself enough? But these are idle questions, for the reason that, where there is any intensity of regard, expression in some form is inevitable for a psycho-physical being, and, moreover, expression is valuable. Let us consider this more closely.

II

In the recognition of worth there is an emotional factor, and it is in connexion with this emotional factor that expression is of especial value. Practical experiment should convince us that there is a reciprocity between an emotion and its outward expression. There is no need to be an adherent of the Lange–James theory of the emotions to agree to this. William James, it will be recalled, maintained that it is our bodily actions which determine our emotions, and not our emotions which determine our actions. According to him we do not cry because we are sad, but we are sad because we cry. This is perverse; but there is a measure of truth in it which we may set out in the two following propositions : (1) the expression of an emotion tends to strengthen the sentiment with which it is associated, and (2) going through the outward acts which are the normal expression of an emotion tends to arouse that emotion even when it is dormant. (The next time you have a fit of the blues, deliberately shape your muscles to a face-splitting smile, and notice the effect.)

The practical value of these principles should be evident. The first, viz., that the expression of an emotion tends to strengthen the sentiment with which it is associated, may be illustrated by recalling a pregnant saying of Baron von Hügel's : ' I kiss my child ', he wrote, ' not only because I love it; I kiss it also in order to love it.' *

The usefulness of the second principle is clear, because, as Prof. J. B. Pratt points out,† acts may be controlled voluntarily and directly, whereas moods have to be tackled in an indirect way.

These considerations have a bearing on the question of specific expression in worship. It would seem to follow from them that, where there is high value in the object of regard, where there is value to the worshipper in the recognition of worth, there is sound reason for such specific expression of regard as will arouse or intensify the emotion which accompanies that recognition.

Specific expression of regard is, then, reasonable, and there are good grounds for employing it deliberately. Often, however, we do not need grounds for employing it; we cannot help ourselves. Fall in love, and you will be hard put to it to suppress the impulse to give expression to your sense of worth (and how idiotic it would be to try !). And why does a man write a letter, and probably send a present, on his mother's birthday? Surely she knows he loves her?

* *Essays and Addresses on the Philosophy of Religion,* p. 251. † *The Religious Consciousness,* p. 281.

Expression, when it really represents the orientation of the personality, is never ' mere ' expression, but is always at the same time a factor in the consolidation of the personality. It accomplishes something. Sometimes it happens spontaneously as a result of the emotional tension of the moment. It may, however, be an activity deliberately undertaken because of its value in strengthening a *sentiment* of regard, and not because of a temporary lively excitement of the feelings. Thus a man's love of his mother is not an emotion, but a sentiment, and a sentiment, as Mr. Shand has shown us, is an organization of a number of different emotional dispositions.* A man's love of his mother is something which persists even when attention is concentrated on interests bearing no relation to her, and it is capable of giving rise to strong emotions differing widely in character (e.g., tender, joyful, wrathful) according to circumstances. When he sits down to write the birthday letter, very likely he is not actuated by any strong emotion; but it would be strange if this act giving expression to his sentiment of love did not excite in him some emotion, this emotion, in turn, strengthening the sentiment. In human relationships such as this there is, of course, a double value in expression, for not

* Cf. *The Foundations of Character*, Bk. I., ch. v.

only is the son's sentiment of love for his mother strengthened, but also her sentiment for him. On receipt of his letter emotion within the sphere of her sentiment of love for him is aroused in her, and it, in turn, strengthens the sentiment.

From the foregoing illustration we see that expression of a sense of worth (i.e. worship) given deliberately, and not under the influence of strong feeling, is, on the human plane, of definite value in adding richness of content to life.

III

What has been said above raises a question of considerable importance in the discussion of religious worship. When a human being gives expression to his sense of the Divine worth does anything happen at ' God's end ' analogous to the enrichment of the mother's sentiment of love for her son? Obviously we shall land ourselves in philosophical absurdities if we say that God's sentiment of love for him is strengthened, and this for at least two reasons. Firstly, God, the Ground of that person's being, cannot be under the necessity of acquiring knowledge about him, and therefore this man's expression (his worship) cannot add any assurance of regard which could strengthen, as between two human beings, mutual estimation. And secondly, for Christian theism at least, God is Love. To be Love admits of no degrees. It is nonsense to speak of the intensification of God's sentiment of love towards someone. Is there any sense, then, in which we may think of a 'difference' being made to God? I believe that there is.

We have seen that expression by arousing emotion in connexion with a sentiment tends to strengthen and intensify that sentiment. Now in worshipping God a man is turning himself towards the highest values; in the measure that he is strengthening and consolidating the supreme sentiment, love to God, he is building up his personality according to the pattern which is God's will for him and which constitutes his perfect goal. It was to this end, the perfection of his personality, that he was created. As he moves towards it he is fulfilling God's purpose, God's meaning for him, the reason for which he has been given freedom to differentiate between good and evil, and to choose. In view of this process and its effect upon the worshipper there would seem, therefore, to be a sense in which we may legitimately speak of God being 'enriched' by the worship; for through this worship His purposes are brought to fruition. In a universe

where God allows a measure of freedom to
finite personalities His purposes may be in
some degree forwarded or frustrated, and we
seem bound to infer that to Him who is love
it does make a ' difference ' whether the one
or the other happens.

There is real weight in this argument, I
think; and yet perhaps in its rationalism it
misses much of the truth. Let us set the
question again, and approach it from another
angle.

How can worship be well-pleasing to God?
How can it be sense to regard Him as desiring
our worship? What difference does it make to
Him?

Children love to bring gifts. A child rushes
into his father's room with some trivial thing—
perhaps some crude object he has cut out or
drawn, perhaps some little belonging of his—
and he earnestly presses it on his father to
keep. Why is the father ' well-pleased ' with
this act? The gift itself is of no use—indeed,
very likely it is rather an embarrassment. If
he analysed his feeling he might attribute it
partly to the indication that his child was
thoughtful of others, and partly to the thought
that this behaviour was expressing and strengthening a sentiment of affection between them.
But surely such an analysis, while possibly

sound in a measure, would be wholly inadequate, and would miss the heart of the experience. I suggest that the essential reason why the father is 'well-pleased' is because this living thing, the warm child-impulse expressing itself in abandoned fervour towards the father—this quality of personal relationship—is something very lovely in and for itself. In the last resort it cannot be analysed. It is beautiful, good— and the heart 'leaps up'. That is all there is to be said.

This propensity of the warm child-heart to bring gifts is a propensity common also to the maturer human being when he is moved by affection. It is compulsive in religion. When a man awakes to the quickening touch of the grace and love of God, there is one question which arises spontaneously to his lips : 'What shall I render unto the Lord?' That is his inevitable response. It is useless to challenge it, and to suggest that it is a foolish question. The effect of the realization of grace and love on a human being is to set him burning to make some return. He cannot help it.

And yet, what return can he make to God? The human child may conceivably be able to give to the human parent a gift which did not come originally from that parent, and which he would not otherwise possess. But what real gift can we bring to Him whose are all the gifts? What can we give that is not already His own, first and all the time?

The reader will recall the words of Psalm li. 15 f. (E.V.; Heb. 17 f.)

> O Lord, open thou my lips;
> And my mouth shall shew forth thy praise.
> For thou delightest not in sacrifice; else would I
>   give it :
> Thou hast no pleasure in burnt offering.

Luther, commenting on this passage, puts these words into God's mouth : 'If I have given you these things, why do you return them to me, as if I had need of them, or as if I required them of you?' And Luther adds : 'The only return which we are able to make to God is to thank him. . . . It is he who strengthens us by his Spirit, who opens our mouth to fill it with praises.' *

The only gift which is ours alone to bring is a direction of spirit. It expresses itself in thanksgiving, the content of which is His, but the will to which is ours. It involves the surrender of ourselves in praiseful submission; and, because in us of ourselves there is shadow and darkness and He is glorious light, it involves also what the psychologists call 'negative self-feeling' (which is, indeed, implied in the very term

* Quoted Will, *Le Culte*, Vol. I., p. 107.

' submission '). And yet, on the contrary, the act is accompanied also by supreme ' positive self-feeling ', for there can be no more positive self-affirmation than a genuine outburst of thanksgiving, and when that thanksgiving is directed towards the Divine in whom alone is the self's fulfilment, the personality is raised to its highest dignity. This may be paradoxical, but it is a paradox of experience. The Psalm from which I have quoted proceeds in verse 17 (Heb. 19) :

> ' The sacrifices of God are a broken spirit :
> A broken and a contrite heart,
> O God, thou wilt not despise.'

The mood of ' and my mouth shall shew forth thy praise ' in verse 15 and the mood of ' a broken and a contrite heart ' in verse 17 seem in marked contrast, and yet the two do in fact combine in the complex, though unified, emotional condition of a man in his approach to God in worship.

Now this gift of thanksgiving, with the direction of spirit which is implied in it, may surely be well-pleasing to God—it may ' make a difference ' to Him—because it is a necessary condition to the birth of a personal relationship of a quality intrinsically lovely and good. The gift is more than a token of an inward disposition of spirit; it is a necessary factor in the creation of a relationship of a particular quality between the Divine Father and His human child. If it were a mere token it might be dispensed with from God's point of view, so to speak, for it would be, to Him, just a signal of what He, all-seeing and all-knowing, knew beforehand; but it is a creative act, it is the one real gift which (always within God's providence, of course) man may bring to God—real in the sense of something which might be withheld, and, being withheld, God would 'lack' something which He 'desired'.

> God doth not need
> Either man's work or his own gifts, who best
> Bear his milde yoak, they serve him best, his state
> Is Kingly.

Milton is right: God doth not 'need' anything of man, save man himself. Even the power to give or to withhold that gift is in the last resort of God's gift; but it is a real freedom, a power given by God to man, in the exercise of which man may 'enrich' even God Himself, or, contrariwise, 'deprive' Him.

IV

It may be objected that this language is figurative, that I am applying terms suitable

to our human and finite experience to the
Divine and Infinite, and that the disparity
between human and divine, finite and infinite,
is so complete that the validity of the application may seriously be called in question. To
this it must be answered that the language
certainly is figurative, for only in figurative
language is it possible for a finite mind to speak
of the infinite, and, indeed, only figuratively
can it think of it. Our thought of the Divine
must be analogical; our finitude makes that
inevitable. But, unless we are prepared to
abandon not only all theology but also all
religion, save the worship of a great mark of
interrogation (and what is there in a question-
mark to evoke worship?), we are bound to
assume that our analogies may be in some
measure valid figurings of eternal Truth.

This is not the place to deal with the ultimate
scepticism about religion. We have to start
with some premiss; and a discussion of the
theory of Christian Worship which hopes to be
profitable will take for granted the Christian
faith (and not exclusively Christian faith either)
that it is possible for a human being to come
into communion with God. For most of us
(and in this we are accompanied by an un-
numbered host of the great and good) our
deepest experiences, and such as seem to be

most surely marked with the accent of truth, make that faith one of which we cannot be rid without being dishonest with life as it meets us.

The point to be made here, however, is that faith in God and in the possibility of communion with Him implies thought about Him, and that that thought must be figurative and analogical. Language which describes accurately human emotions and human relationships cannot be transferred to God with an identical signification, but yet it may be the most adequate human means available of shadowing forth the truth about God. When a positive attribute is applied to God, the question to ask is not whether the terms used are in every respect accurate, but whether they are the most adequate approximation to the truth which human thought and language can supply.

If the reader is inclined to think that reliance on analogical description and analogical inference leads naturally to the desert of agnosticism, let him consider how dependent we are on just these processes both for the acquisition of knowledge and for the proclamation of truth within the sphere of purely human experience. Think, for instance, of the word ' riches ', the primary signification of which is material wealth. To the modern mind it will summon up thoughts of coins and cheques and bank-balances; in a more primitive state of society the first thoughts would be of flocks and herds, of vines and fig trees. Now consider the two statements : ' the company promoter was enriched by the transaction ' and 'the musician was enriched by listening to the performance of Beethoven's Fifth Symphony '. In the one ' enriched ' means ' provided with riches ' in the primary sense of material wealth; in the other it means ' provided with riches ' in a spiritual sense. This spiritual wealth is not a form of material wealth; it is something wholly different. We call it a ' possession ', but it is not a possession as we may talk of a sovereign or a cow being a possession; it might be described more accurately as a modification of the personality through experience. Yet, in order to convey this subtle spiritual effect which the hearing of the symphony has had on the musician, we have to borrow a word which belongs properly to a different and lower order of experience, and we say he was ' enriched '. Suppose you were to try to explain to a philistine company promoter, who knew little of music and cared less, what the Fifth Symphony meant to the musician, you would presumably convey some notion of it by telling him that the musician felt the ' richer ' for his experience. He would appreciate that you were speaking figuratively, and that you did not mean that the musician imagined himself to have more treasury notes in his pocket. For this particular man the analogy implied in the term ' richer ' would convey some measure of the sense of value and worth found in the experience. The experience itself would continue to be something beyond him, and yet his own experience would be enlarged to the extent of a faint apprehension not only of the existence, but also of the nature, of an order of experience of which he had been hitherto entirely ignorant. By means of analogy he would have reached out from the known to the unknown, and so doing he would have grown in knowledge. And notice this : if the figure had been stressed in its primary significance it would have been positively misleading, and yet, on the other hand, the fuller the value given to it as a conveyer of meaning by analogy the nearer would it have brought the company promoter to an apprehension of the truth.

This illustration has its obvious defects, partly because the concept of spiritual enrichment is so common that the word ' enrich ' may call it up straight away without reference to material riches, and partly because it would be impossible to find even a philistine company

c

promoter who had had no experience of an
' enrichment ' which was not material. Yet it
may serve to remind us of how dependent we
are upon figures drawn from a lower order of
experience in order to communicate the higher
and subtler experiences of the spirit. We cannot enter into the experience of God any more
than our fictitious company promoter could
enter into the experience of the musician, but
we can faintly apprehend that God may be
affected in a manner which finds its nearest
human analogy in an enrichment which is at
once spiritual and personal.

v

Let us return now to our main theme. We
have, I believe, brought to light what is the
essential act of religious worship, and also why
it is a duty. The essential act of worship is
the BRINGING OF A GIFT. Its obligation lies in
this : that, the nature of human personality
being what it is, the act of giving is an essential
factor, on the human side, in the creation of
the relationship between God and man which
God most desires.

Here is a fundamental principle which must
guide all subsequent discussion. It is at once
age-long and revolutionary. It is age-long,

because the classical expression of worship has always been sacrifice; it is revolutionary, because—well, how many commonly give any thought to it when they go to church?

It is idle to discuss the rival merits of different kinds and forms of worship until we know what constitutes an act of worship. That essential constituent is Giving. Unless the act is first and foremost one of giving, of offering, it has no right to be called an act of worship. Of course, vastly more than the mere offering is involved in worship : communion with God, the effect on the worshipper individually and in his social relations of contact with the Divine, and so on. These all go to making the importance of worship supreme. They are, however, the concomitants and consequences of worship. They intensify the urge to it; they make of it an activity abounding in blessing to the worshipper; but they are not the worship itself.

Who would guess from our church notice-boards or, alas, from a great number of our services, that when a man comes really to worship, he comes first and foremost to bring an offering to God, and that it is the chief function (though not the only function) of a service of public worship to help him and all gathered with him to make a worthy offering?

But we are anticipating. So far we have considered only the general nature of religious worship and the claim of this worship on the individual. The proof of the need for corporate worship requires a chapter to itself.

| Chapter | The Claim of |
| III | Corporate Worship |

I

ALL religions which have survived to be recorded in history have possessed some sort of cult, some way of corporate worship. The cult, says a French scholar, is the combination (or aggregate) of practices whereby the particular religion (la foi) is made known and renews its life.* It is by means of the cult, says another writer, that religions declare both their existence and their intention to last (de durer). Without it not one of them could be maintained.†

Is this final statement true? The modern revolt against anything which might be called 'institutional religion', in which many share who would not disclaim the name of Christian, implies the assumption that it is false. True

* 'Le culte est l'ensemble des pratiques par lesquelles la foi s'exprime et se recrée.' Henri Delacroix, *La Religion et la Foi*, p. 15.

† Robert Will, *Le Culte*, Vol. II., p. 26.

religion, men say, is a concern between the soul and God. It is something intimate and personal, and the restrictions and formality of corporate worship are a hindrance, not a help, to this 'immediate' commerce. Presumably, then, they will be inclined to think that however right the historians may be in affirming that hitherto no religion has survived without a cult, yet they are not justified in asserting that no religion could survive without one. Does not the highest religion preclude a cult? Has the highest no survival value? This line of thought requires careful scrutiny. That true religion is a concern between the soul and God no thinking Christian would deny, but the facile conclusion that this proposition implies an extreme individualism in the highest reaches of religion is not demanded by the premiss.

II

We may recall first of all that the relation between God and the human soul is socially conditioned. The individual rapt in adoring contemplation of God is dependent upon his fellow-men for the possibility of the vision which evokes his adoration. Like the scientist who has made a new discovery, he may see what others have not seen before him; but just as the scientist's discovery is dependent upon the vast body of knowledge acquired by others and handed on to him, so his deeper vision is possible only because other seers before him have enabled him to start better equipped to see further.

The Christian in his most private devotions speaks to, and hears speaking to him, a God who is conceived ethically and personally in terms of Jesus Christ. In his thought of God he cannot get away from those qualities which Jesus represents. They colour his conception of the God to whom he is addressing himself, and they colour the messages which are God's return to the outgoing of his heart. It is idle to suppose that God reveals Himself in all that we may call His ' Jesus qualities ' apart from Jesus. There is no shred of evidence that He does, and if He could, it would be hard to see that Jesus had any necessary place in history— and if that life and that death were superfluous our very faith in the righteousness of God would be shaken. But the Lord Jesus who thus conditions the Christian's highest apprehensions of God is Himself socially mediated to the Christian who has found Him. Apart from the Christian community which from generation to generation has treasured Him as its most precious possession we should be unable to find Him, and we should lack that revelation of God which is the presupposition of our most exalted acts of personal communion.

In reply to this it may be said that doubtless the Christian community has in the past been a vital necessity, but that, in this particular regard at all events, it has performed its task. Jesus is mediated to us through the New Testament. It is true that without the Church there would have been no New Testament; it is true that without the Church it would not have survived through the centuries to the age of printing; but now it is available for any seeker after God who may desire to profit by it. For the religious man it has become a classic. The churches—the organized bodies of Christians—may indeed make the sales larger than they would be without them, but if they ceased to exist the publishers would not cease to publish. The publication of the New Testament is now no more dependent upon institutional religion than is the publication of the works of Shakespeare on the existence of a Shakespeare Society.

This argument lacks cogency on account of its hypothetical nature, but its radical weakness is that it rests on an inadequate analysis of actual religious experience. It is not only through the pages of the New Testament that the Lord Jesus is mediated to us. He is also mediated through living Christian people. This is as true for the vast majority of those who will have nothing to do with organized Christianity as it is for the church-goers. A man may eschew parsons and pews, but, unless he abandons his religion altogether (in which event he has nothing to do with the present argument), he cannot escape from his debt to the mother who taught him his ' first fond prayers ' or to this and that individual who kindled or fed the flame of Christ-reverence in his heart. Moreover, the law which applies to our endeavours to apprehend the external world applies also to our dealings with, and understanding of, the New Testament : ' to him that hath shall be given '. We receive in the measure that we bring. Our knowledge of the external world is of something ' given ', and yet our acquiring of it involves at all points a process of interpretation, and the fullness of our knowing is dependent upon what we can bring in the way of mental powers and of a well-stored mind. That does not mean that what we call the external world is merely a ' projection ' of our own minds. We are dealing with ' facts ', with things ' given '; and woe betide us if we play fast and loose with what is given. But the ' given ' is not like a Christmas present neatly tied up in

a parcel, so that we have only to cut the string
and unwrap the paper, and there we are. It
is more like a vast organ, the potential vehicle
of many-coloured sounds. One man comes to
it, and is baffled by this unintelligible, dumb
thing. Another comes a little better equipped;
he experiments with the ' voice ' and ' timbre '
of the various stops, singly and in combination,
and apprehends some small measure of the
significance of the instrument by playing simple
chords and formless successions of notes with
one hand on a key-board. Another scrambles
and stumbles through a ' slow movement ' with
hands and feet; while yet another, after a little
quiet contemplation of the instrument, is soon
off and away, lost to earth in the surging
immensities of a Bach fugue. To each of these
men that organ is a ' fact ', something quite
specific, with definite limitations; but the
difference between what it gives to one and to
another is beyond calculation. ' To him that
hath shall be given.'

This principle applies to our apprehension of
the divine message in the New Testament. It
is thither that we turn to find the Lord Jesus.
He is presented to us in those pages, and if it
is Jesus whom we seek, and not some figment
of our imagination, we must always be dealing
with that presentation. But is the Figure

there portrayed intelligible and meaningful *in the same way* to everyone who reads and re-reads those books? Obviously not. For instance, is there no difference between the Jesus that was apprehended by St. Francis and the Jesus that is apprehended by Dr. Albert Schweitzer? And are we going to say that, because of the manifest difference, therefore one of them can never have touched Him at all, if indeed either of them has? That would surely be folly.

Our mental and spiritual background must affect our insight for better or for worse (often, no doubt, in some respects for better, while in other respects for worse). Christianity is a living religion. The Christian who turns to the New Testament has had in his own life experience of what he confidently asserts to be the divine. Inevitably he brings that experience to his interpretation of the New Testament narrative. And there are sources of help beyond his own personal, practical experience. Others there are to whom the things of Christ are a living reality—men and women whose lives confess a harmonizing assurance of a depth to which he probably could lay no claim. They too can help him to bring a finer discernment to his reading and meditation.

Most of us are brought to the records of the

43

Master in the New Testament by Christian people. We go to these records, and, as we think and contemplate and absorb, our souls are quickened, and we find ourselves possessed of an ever more wonderful inheritance. But it is a mistake to suppose that what is going on, and what brings about this result, is simply a commerce between ourselves and a written historical narrative. The wells of the New Testament never run dry because they are shafts sunk to an eternal Spring : God speaking in his Son. But what we draw is dependent on what we bring, and the vessel that we let down is large according as its making is of the construction of the Christian brotherhood, and not merely our own. It is vain to attempt to separate what we learn of Christ from the Gospels from what we learn of Him from those whose experience has been of Him. The two sources are complementary. Each checks the other, each illuminates the other.*

The relation between God and the human soul is, then, socially conditioned. That is a most important truth, and the realization of it would save many from much self-imposed spiritual poverty. It shows (if any demonstration is needed) the importance of Christians associating

* Of course, even the Gospels are in a measure ' interpretations ' based on experience.

together and the folly of deliberate isolation.
It is not, however, of itself sufficient to prove
the necessity of corporate *worship*. This
necessity is to be found in a further truth, not
unconnected with the foregoing, the truth,
namely, that the primitive and classical Christian experience is a *social* experience.

III

' After this manner therefore pray ye : Pater
NOSTER . . . Adveniat REGNUM tuum
. . .'' * Thus the New Testament tells us our
Lord taught his disciples to pray; thus have
his disciples continuously prayed for nineteen
centuries. It is no mere accident that the
pattern prayer of Christians is prayed in the
plural. Jesus preached a kingdom,—which on
any reading is a social entity. It is quite true
that the chief reference in the New Testament
usage of the word ' kingdom ' (or, more fully,
the phrases ' kingdom of God ' and ' kingdom
of heaven ') is a reference Godwards rather than
fellow-manwards; it is primarily the ' rule '
or ' sovereignty ' of God, the main thought
being on the kingly rule, and not on the corporate
association of those ruled.† But at the same

* Mt. vi. 9 ff.

† Cf. Dalman, *The Words of Jesus*, E.T., pp. 91–147, and
Headlam, *The Doctrine of the Church and Reunion*, p. 19.

time there is a social element in the concept, always at least implicit and sometimes, as for instance in the parables of the Mustard Seed and the Leaven, brought into prominence.* Moreover, the Sovereign Lord into whose rule we are called to enter is ' our Father ', and the correlative of ὁ πατὴρ ἡμῶν, ' our Father ', is ἀδελφοί, ' brethren '.

This word ἀδελφοί, as applying to the Christian community, haunts the New Testament. To become a ' son ' means to enter into a ' brotherhood '—I Peter gives us the very word: ἡ ἀδελφότης, the brotherhood,—*fraternitas*, as the Vulgate renders it.† Another word —' fellowship ' ‡—indicates this very prominent feature of primitive Christian experience. It is a fellowship so close that Paul speaks of Christians as members together of one body : ' we, who are many, are one body in Christ, and severally members one of another '.§ The Christian life was one of sharing in, of being partakers together of, the heavenly rule.¶ So it was in the early days, and so it must be. In the things of the spirit we grow rich by sharing.

* Cf. Headlam, op. cit., pp. 20 ff.
† I Peter ii. 17; v. 9.
‡ κοινωνία. Vid. e.g., Acts ii. 42, Phil. i. 5, I Jn. i. 3–7.　　　§ Rom. xii. 5.　　　¶ Cf. Rev. i. 9.

The Claim of Corporate Worship

Herein lies the necessity of corporate worship. As we saw in the previous chapter, God can be recognized only in worship, for it is in the act of ascribing to him absolute worth that we know him to be God. This is as true for the group as for the individual. The corporate recognition of him within the social group implies corporate worship. The Christian experience of God is a social as well as an individual experience, and the 'communion of saints' necessitates common worship.

Certainly there are experiences which call forth the response of worship from the individual alone to God, and where the desire for the company of other Christians does not form part of that response; but this surely is not true of the distinctively social experiences connected with membership of the Kingdom. Here the individual is moved to worship because of what has come to him as a member of a community, and it is as a member of this community that he is moved to 'laud and magnify' God's glorious name not only with the saints below, but with the saints above—with angels and archangels and all the company of heaven. 'Ye are come unto mount Zion, and unto the city of the living God, the heavenly Jerusalem, and to innumerable hosts of angels, to the general assembly and church of the firstborn who are enrolled in heaven, and to God the Judge of all, and to the spirits of just men made perfect, and to Jesus the mediator of a new covenant, and to the blood of sprinkling that speaketh better than that of Abel. . . . Wherefore, receiving a kingdom that cannot be shaken, let us have grace [or perhaps better ' gratitude '] whereby we may offer service well-pleasing to God with reverence and awe.' (Heb. xii. 22–24, 28.) He who has caught a glimpse of this vision which the author of the Epistle to the Hebrews has described with such poetic insight and fervour will never be content to confine himself to private worship in the sole company of ' Dr. Greenfield '.

Corporate worship is, then, inevitable if the Christian life is to be lived in the richness of which it is capable. We can, indeed, go further, and say, as the scholars quoted at the beginning of the chapter imply, that it is inevitable if in the long run the faith is to be maintained at all. For the faith is socially mediated, and that mediation is the outcome of a social experience of God, an experience which implies social worship.

The Claim of Corporate Worship

To the reasoning of the foregoing section the reader will perhaps object that, logical as it may sound, it simply does not fit in with the facts. Are there not admirable Christians—more admirable indeed than the majority of those who associate themselves with ' organized religion '—who never assemble themselves for worship with their fellow-Christians, and whose lives do not seem to be impoverished by the omission? The answer to that question is that there may be, but even if there are it does not invalidate the argument. There are men in affluent circumstances who have never had to earn their living; but that does not disprove the law that in the last resort wealth always depends upon work.

This book is concerned with public worship. Corporate worship is not public worship unless the public has free access to it. There is no need, however, to devote long paragraphs to proving the propriety of making the meetings for worship public. Christianity is a missionary religion; it cannot flourish under conditions where it enjoys its own treasures regard-

D 49

less of the deprivation of those outside. The true Zion is a city set on a hill.

VI

If our argument hitherto has been sound we have shown the necessity of corporate worship as the spontaneous reaction of the group to its corporate apprehension of God. But obviously it is a considerable jump from such spontaneous behaviour to the formality of the cult as it is found in the different Christian communions. So far we have not proved the desirability, let alone the necessity, of any sort of formal ' Service '. This will be the theme of the next chapter.

Chapter IV

An Artificial Element
Necessary in the Cult

I

IT was argued in the preceding chapter that
Christian experience implies the Christian
group, and that corporate worship is the spontaneous and necessary reaction of the group to
its corporate apprehension of God. At first
sight that might seem to suggest that a cult in
any formal sense is hardly required. Let Christians meet together to share their experiences
of God; that is enough, and corporate worship
will automatically ensue. A little reflexion,
however, will show that a group which is to
survive must, in the nature of things social,
organize itself and its activities. This at once
introduces an element into its proceedings which
is formal and not spontaneous. For instance,
if the group is to be a real group capable of
sharing, and not merely an assembly of isolated
and unrelated units, the ' spontaneity ' of the
individual must be subordinated to the needs
of the whole. This subordination cannot be
relied upon to occur of itself, witness the

behaviour of the church at Corinth as described by St. Paul.* There must be some regulation and control—some artificiality, in fact. How is it that Friends find themselves shaking hands at the close of a ' Meeting for Worship ' punctually to the hour? Lovers are notoriously unmindful of the clock; and it would be curious if wholly unregulated worship conformed spontaneously to the hour-glass.

The formal element in corporate worship, however, cannot be confined to regulations respecting time and place and the observance of decent social conventions between members of the group. All social communication depends upon the formal and conventional. This is manifest in the realms not only of art and literature but also of science. The vast edifice of modern science is preserved from immediate disintegration because it is consolidated with the mortar of artificial symbols. The conventional is the great preservative of scientific experience, and it is no less so of religious experience.

This consideration has a bearing on the function of the Christian cult in the modern world. A little group of Christians living in a small town may meet together regularly in, let us say, a schoolroom to share the fruits of their religious experience and to seek God's face.

* I Cor. xiv.

An Artificial Element Necessary in the Cult

If they be honest persons and serious ' professors ' of Christ, their lives will be enriched by the common sharing, and, moreover, they will achieve corporate worship. That would be valuable, and all to the good; but if they thus confined themselves to their own limited circle of experience they would be contenting themselves with a spiritual poverty quite unnecessary to a Christian living in the 20th century. There is a world-wide and age-long inheritance which is theirs to enter, and they fall far short of the possibilities open to them if they do not seek to share in this vaster wealth available.

If the cult is to serve as a medium for the conveyance of this wider experience, clearly its structure must be in large measure formal and artificial, for it can perform this task only by symbolical representation. It is therefore bound to become a work of art. Its effectiveness will be according as it succeeds in expressing these things of the spirit, but it can express them so that they become living only through the formal and conventional. Dr. Will has put the point in a happy epigram. ' Certainly ', he says, ' form without spirit is dead, but spirit without form is not capable of living.' *

* ' Certes, la forme sans l'esprit est morte, mais l'esprit sans la forme n'est pas viable.' *Le Culte*, Vol. II., p. 31.

This principle is of paramount importance in relation to public worship. Failure to recognize it clearly, and to work out its implications, is a chief cause of weakness in the Free Churches at the present day. Their traditional practice in the last analysis assumes the principle; but in more recent years they have shown signs of denying it. They have felt uneasy about the formal, suspecting it of being opposed to the spiritual; and God is to be worshipped in spirit and in truth. Consequently they have become slipshod in the formal elements of a service in the hopes of making them appear as informal as possible. But this is foolish. If the formal is undesirable it should be abolished, not camouflaged. Logically their theory demands a meeting of the Quaker type as the nearest practical approximation to the ideal. The formal frame-work of a Free Church service is merely an encumbrance unless the form is a necessary medium for the effective expression of the spiritual.

A composer who is true in his soul will not write a symphony unless he feels the symphonic form to be the best means of expressing the musical values which he is seeking to express; but once he feels it to be the right medium, the means by which he can say best what he wants to say, he will submit himself without regret to the limitations it imposes, and he will know that the success of his expression will be bound up with his success in perfecting the form which he has adopted. What success he achieves will not be in spite of the form but because of it. Similarly Christians are justified in adopting a mode of Service only if their medium is one which they can delight in as good.

II

Go to a service in any church or chapel you choose, and you will be present at an activity which is artificial, that is, the behaviour of the assembled people will not be spontaneous. No 'service' that one can think of would simply 'happen' as it does if the people came together to worship without any conventions to observe or preconceived modes of procedure to follow. That might seem to be a serious indictment of the services, for untruth in religion is intolerable, and we are inclined to think of the artificial as of something at least a little false. But there is one kind of artificiality which may be wholly subservient to the truth, and that is the artificiality of art.

As a form a sonnet is highly artificial, but it may serve as a perfect means of expressing certain values. It served as a 'key' with which

55

' Shakespeare unlock'd his heart '; in the hand of Milton it

> ' became a trumpet; whence he blew
> Soul-animating strains—alas, too few ! '

And will it be held that what Wordsworth said in his two sonnets on ' The Sonnet ' could have been expressed as effectively by any less formal means?

In art form is the handmaid of truth. Form in public worship is in need of no defence when it is an essential element in the expression through art of spiritual things.

Professor W. L. Sperry indicates the ultimate justification of formal public worship when he says, ' A service of public worship is an artistic recapitulation of Christian experience '. ' This experience ', he continues, ' has a double aspect. It is, in the first place, the experience of the single individual coming from the solitude of his own disciplines and struggles to a place where he may find perfect self-expression. It is, in the second place, the experience of two thousand Christian years and many Christian generations as that experience is reconsidered, revised, and restated. The service of public worship is an affirmation of that which the church holds to be permanently valid and true in Christian history as a whole.' *

> * *Reality in Worship*, p. 175.

An Artificial Element Necessary in the Cult

If, then, in a public service we are moving in the realms of art, it follows that form and structure must be given due consideration; they must be worthy and fit for their task, and they must be regarded as such. If, on the other hand, to think of a service in terms of art is to misconceive the nature of right corporate worship, then the structure of a so-called 'free' Nonconformist service and the structure of a high and dignified liturgy are equally indefensible. The issue here is a plain one, and we must make up our minds on it.

III

A service of public worship an artistic recapitulation of Christian experience : we shall consider presently some of the implications of this view, but first it is necessary to insist that it does not mean what would be popularly meant by the plea for more 'art' in public worship. It does not constitute a demand for beautiful buildings, for better-trained choirs, for more 'colour', expressed, for instance, in vestments or pictures or stained-glass windows, nor for more dramatic movement. These things may or may not be generally desirable, or desirable in particular circumstances, but it would be possible to have them all and yet be as far off as ever from exemplifying the principle enunciated. The work of art required is the work of art which expresses the vital values of Christian experience, and which expresses them so that they may be apprehended by the particular group of worshippers. 'Art' seems the right word to describe what we mean, for we are contemplating the symbolical embodiment of values which gives rise to an experience which is in itself satisfying, just as an æsthetic experience is in itself satisfying. While this is true, it must nevertheless be recognized that the object of a service as a work of art differs in an important respect from the object of, let us say, a picture or a sonata or an ode as a work of art. Perhaps the distinction is best expressed by saying that while the object of the latter is an æsthetic experience—an experience of beauty —the object of the former is a religious experience—an experience of God. I do not mean, of course, that an æsthetic experience cannot be an experience of God, nor even that there can be an experience of God wholly lacking an æsthetic attribute; yet, while the distinction is not absolute, it is one which needs to be made.

An illustration will, perhaps, make the point clearer. It will hardly be denied that some of our Lord's parables are consummate works of art: gems of the imagination, perfect in their expressiveness. They may be contemplated 'æsthetically' for the sheer beauty of their form and content and for the perfect fitness and conformity of the one to the other. In the character of 'artist' Jesus would have found all the satisfaction he needed in the act of expression, in the very creation of a piece of perfectly embodied meaning; yet we can be quite certain that they were not composed primarily either for that satisfaction or for the æsthetic enjoyment of his hearers. Using colloquial language, we may say that the one thing he was concerned to do was to 'get over' a message—a message, in the last resort, about God. Unless I misunderstand the generally accepted views of the theorists in art, such a purpose is held to be inconsistent with the ideals of a genuine artist. Doubtless a true work of art may—indeed, perhaps, must—convey a 'message', but the artist's first business is to express, not to teach, and the message which he conveys is of secondary importance.

A service calls for the skill of an architect, one who is expert at adapting structure to function, and who in the exercise of a utilitarian art produces something which is satisfying in itself. This analogy will serve, it may be, better than any other to show that in the use of the term 'art' I am thinking not of ornamentation, nor primarily of æsthetic value, but of fitness of expression for a clearly defined purpose.

IV

I referred above to the Quaker type of service, and suggested that the theory of many Free Churchmen should lead logically to this. So far as my observation goes, the younger Nonconformists of to-day who still hold to 'organized religion' are little satisfied with the traditional Free Church service, and they are attracted either towards the richer kind of Anglicanism to be found now or towards Quakerism, according to temperament. This double movement away from the Free Churches * is in the main a 'cult' movement. The younger generation is not very interested in theological dogma, and it is almost wholly uninterested in principles of church government. What it is concerned about in the sphere of organized religion is to find a cult which is spiritually satisfying.

* For convenience I am excluding the Society of Friends from this category in the present argument. It is, of course, a nonconformist body, and it is also Free Church in a sense which cannot be applied to another great nonconformist body in this country, namely the Roman Catholic Church.

An Artificial Element Necessary in the Cult

Let us examine the claims of the Quaker mode of Worship. Dr. H. H. Brinton in his admirable little book *Creative Worship* * sets them out cogently, and it will be convenient to follow his exposition.

V

At the outset it may be noted that he has very little favourable to say for what he calls Protestant or Puritan modes of worship. The Roman Mass he can appreciate, even if he cannot subscribe to the Roman theory which gives the Mass its supreme value; it is essentially worship. The corporate mysticism of the Quaker Meeting is essentially worship. Protestant services, on the other hand, are not essentially worship. To these last, however, there is one exception : the Communion Service. The Puritan, he admits, attains to real worship where the Communion is not only a symbol, but also a mystic rite which enables the communicant to share in the life of Christ. How far Dr. Brinton is justified in his view we shall try to consider. For the moment I would draw attention to the fact that the Quaker scholar writing of Christian worship finds what can

* Swarthmore Lecture, 1931.

most unequivocally be called worship in the
Mass, the Communion, and the Friends' Meeting. He finds it, in short, in the Communion,
for the Quaker Meeting for worship is also in
ideal a Communion.

True worship, Dr. Brinton maintains, is an
end in itself; and surely he is right. His count
against the common run of Puritan so-called
services of worship is that they are not looked
upon as ends in themselves, but as means to a
purpose, usually that of promoting ' an improved
type of behaviour '. The worshipper is not
allowed to give himself up to worship; he is
exhorted to do this or to believe that; he is
made to sing hymns of praise, and directed in
the presentation of petitions to the Almighty.
Everything is restless; the tension is never
relaxed; the worshipper must be continually
struggling for that which cannot be achieved
in this life. He may, Dr. Brinton grants,
' become so wrapped in the beauty of music or
ritual that the external goal is at the moment
forgotten. But the sermon eventually makes it
clear that the service is not primarily directed
toward an æsthetic experience. Words, in
Protestant worship, are not goals. They are
tools used to accomplish a purpose, usually to
promote an improved type of behaviour.' *

* Op. cit., p. 41.

The criticism he is making has considerable force, although the account he gives is little other than a caricature of some Puritan services, as he himself would probably be ready to allow. Moreover, it contains no hint that he has any acquaintance with that type of sermon which is perhaps the ideal type in Puritan theory, namely that which is a setting forth of Christ in such wise as to move the congregation to true worship and adoration. And as for his statement that in Protestant worship words are not goals, but tools used to accomplish a purpose, I fail to see why this should cause any misgiving. The ' end ' of a service, on his own showing, should be worshipful communion with God. How are words legitimate except as ' means ' to this ' end '? It can hardly be that he holds that words themselves may be God, although we can readily agree that they may mediate Him to persons living under terrestrial conditions. Further, the objection, if it is an objection, that words in Protestant worship are tools, not goals, may equally be levelled against the lack of words in the Quaker silence; we may with equal truth retort : ' The Silence, in Quaker worship, is not a goal, but a tool to accomplish a purpose ', and I cannot see that it would be a very damaging criticism. Indeed, if it could be said that the Silence was a goal, it would be tantamount to affirming the supreme emptiness of Quaker practice.

Yet the main point for which Dr. Brinton contends is a sound one. It is comparatively rare for the Protestant in his ordinary services to find, or even to look for, an experience which is satisfying in itself and which makes the hour unspeakably worth while quite apart from any ' good ' which may result from it. Real worship does not look to anything beyond. The Psalmist who wrote ' I was glad when they said unto me, Let us go into the house of the Lord ' (cxxii. 1) was not thinking of his pleasure at being given the opportunity of attending a meeting which might make him a better Hebrew ; he was expressing his feeling at the prospect of enjoying a uniquely satisfying experience, as a youthful enthusiast for art might say, ' I was glad when they said unto me, Let us go into the National Gallery '.

' If I meet with a friend whom I love ', writes Dr. Brinton, ' I do not think of the good this meeting will do me. I enjoy the occasion for what it is. I may reflect afterward that the meeting helped me, but at the time I enjoy the moment of common life with my friend as an experience which is beautiful and good in and for itself. In the same way worship which is organic rather than instrumental finds that life shared with God is good in itself. In the silence of all flesh the worshipper turns

> Towards the Uncreated with a countenance
> Of adoration, and with an eye of love.

Inner tension is relaxed. The present moment attains supreme worth. No word of advice, no thought of duty points beyond the instant. The worshipper becomes an organic part of a larger whole of life which is harmonised, complete and at rest.' * That is the sort of experience, he holds, to which the Friends' Meeting for Worship is adapted. The Puritan, on the other hand, he would say, does not as a rule look for anything like that. His whole training is, indeed, against it. His Services reflect his inbred uneasiness with life, his restless ethical striving, and his inability to give himself up in unresisting abandonment to the divine which is here. He has an uncomfortable feeling that he is culpably wasting his time if he allows himself to ' consider the lilies ' beyond a brief glance. He could not regard such a passivity as a means to his moral improvement; and worse, it is not a means to anything. Similarly, he cannot feel his worship to be quite legitimate unless it is a means to something beyond, to his betterment, or his salvation, or the glory of God.

* Op. cit., p. 46 f.

VI

Dr. Brinton contends, then, that the first mark of Quaker worship is that it is ' a goal rather than a process '. Secondly, Quaker worship is ' based on an inner creative life which the Mystics know to be God '. The evidence of this inner creative life is, if I understand him, the harmonizing effect which the period of worship has upon the personality. The worshipper may come ' at odds with himself ', disturbed by all manner of inner conflicts. ' Through prayer, contrition and self-surrender all these are sacrificed on the invisible altar ',* and there ensues in the silence a message of peace. The upshot is that ' the soul of the worshipper is reborn because the warring elements have been harmonised into new life '. † Worship has this effect as no other experience has because ' in worship the life of the individual merges with the Ideal Life '.‡ The soul ' returns to earth but it does not return unchanged. Something of the harmonising principle which seeks to unite the world organically in the bonds of Love has permeated its being.' ' Such worship may be private or public, but in either case it will be in silence for the self assertion of the individual must be stilled if the voice of

* Op. cit., p. 49.   † ibid., p. 50.   ‡ ibid.

the Universal is to be heard.' *   It is of paramount importance that we should listen.   The
new messages given to the world by the great
spiritual leaders have come not because these
men spoke to God, but because they listened
to Him.

Dr. Brinton is not altogether clear in his
exposition of this his second mark of Quaker
worship, although broadly that for which he is
contending seems plain enough.   I fancy that
this aspect of the Quaker way is the one where
it shows itself most weak, in spite of its possess-
ing obvious points of strength.   To this I shall
return.   It will be better to enumerate first the
three remaining marks of Quaker worship which
he distinguishes.

The third is that the Friends' practice ' makes
possible the emergence of the new '.   The
Quaker mode he holds to be far more effective
in this respect than what he calls the ' mechanistic ' worship of Protestantism generally.   The
latter is based on that which is supplied exter-
nally and traditionally, whether ritual, creed,
hymn, Scripture, or sermon.   The former being
' based on the Inner Light which is also the
Inner Life is as open to the novel and unexpected as is life itself.' †   It is not, of course,
that the Friend disclaims historic foundations

* Op. cit., p. 51.   † ibid., p. 55.

to his religion. It is, rather, that he claims to act more in consonance with the Puritan John Robinson's faith that ' the Lord had yet more truth and light to break forth out of his holy Word ' (though the modern Quaker would probably give a much wider connotation than did John Robinson to the phrase ' his holy Word '). Dr. Brinton points out that ' there have been few extensive reforms during the past three centuries which the Society of Friends has not anticipated within its own member-ship ', *e.g.*, thought and practice with regard to peace, the abolition of negro slavery, temper-ance, prison reform, the care of the insane. This, he maintains, is due, not to any intrinsic merit in its members, but to their adoption of ' a form of worship which was especially adapted to the emergence of unforeseen qualities of life '. *

His fourth characteristic of Quaker worship is that it ' binds a group of worshippers into an organic unity '. This condition of organic unity is not always achieved in Meeting, but it is an experience which Friends know well, and there are old Quaker phrases which were (and perhaps still are) employed to indicate that this common life has been realized. ' A gathered meeting ' is one. Another is used in the expres-

* Vid. ibid., p. 56.

sion : there is a 'covering' over the meeting.
The unifying power which directs and har-
monizes the group is called 'the life of the
meeting', and words are said to be spoken 'in
the life of the meeting' when they express in
any way the sentiment of the unified whole.
It should be understood, however, that a meeting may be 'in the life' even though not a
single word has been uttered.* We cannot
begin to understand the hold which the Society
of Friends has on its members until we appreciate in some measure the quality of experience
to which these phrases are appropriate. How
far they go to the heart of Quakerism may be
judged by the fact that Dr. Brinton, searching
for an adequate definition of Quakerism, offers
as the best that he can give : 'the belief that
the highest type of worship is a group mysticism
which affords opportunity for the silent growth
of organic relations uniting the worshippers with
God and with each other.' †

For a Meeting to be transfigured into 'a
gathered meeting' it must be composed (perhaps not exclusively, I should suppose, but at
least almost entirely) of folk whose everyday
life is that of sincere practising Christians. It
is necessary to come prepared. 'We cannot',
writes Dr. Brinton, 'be insensitive to the needs

* Vid. ibid., pp. 70 ff.   † ibid., p. 67.

of our neighbours before meeting and then quickly become sensitive to God and our fellow men in meeting.' And again, ' Worship is an art in which some attain proficiency quickly and others slowly. In either case the success of the meeting is largely dependent on the quality of life which has preceded it.' *

This leads us naturally into his fifth characteristic of Quaker worship, which is that it ' seeks to extend to the entire human race this unity of men with each other and with God '.

However necessary it may be to insist that an act of worship is an end in itself, and not primarily a means to some other good, yet it still remains true that worship cannot be separated from its consequences; and Dr. Brinton holds that the Quaker mode of worship is more far-reachingly Christian in its consequences than either Protestant or Catholic worship. (The phrase is not his, but I think it is fair to his meaning.) This arises out of the difference in nature which he finds between Quaker and other modes of worship. Protestant worship, for instance, as we have seen, he calls ' mechanical ' worship, because it employs means to work from outside upon the worshippers. Scripture, hymn, spoken prayer, sermon—these are as it were so many strokes

* ibid., p. 75.

with the cue to set the spiritual billiard ball, which is the worshipper, on the religious move, and on the move in a certain calculated direction. Quaker worship, on the other hand, is ' organic '; the members of the group are inter-related as are the members of a living organism, so that any movement, whether of prayer or praise or what not, which manifests itself within the group is an expression of this living unity, just as the purposive movement of the hand is the expression of the living organism which we call a person. Moreover, the direction of the movement represents the response of the organism as a whole to its environment; it is not merely a reflex movement compulsively set going by an external stimulus, as the eye blinks when an object is suddenly flicked past it.

Dr. Brinton claims that the effect of ' mechanical ' worship is to emphasize ' mechanical ' relations between men, while that of ' organic ' worship is to emphasize ' organic ' relations. Mechanical relations imply our treating our fellow-men in the same way as we treat physical objects in general, but ' if, through the experience of worship, we have become intensely aware of the possibility of organic relations among men, then we endeavour to create those relations by love which operates from within '.*

* ibid., p. 81.

71

Love is not coercive; it always reverences
personality, giving respect to freedom and
individuality; by self-surrender it attracts others
into the unity of a common life.

The following quotation will, perhaps, set out
in relief his view regarding the superiority of
Quakerism. ' The Protestant ', he writes, ' has
inherited a tradition which finds man to be
" natural " and permits him to act in a " natural "
way [cf. war]; the Catholic finds man to be
" natural " in the world and spiritual in the
Church and therefore gives him a double code
of behaviour; the Quaker believes that he must
act as if he and all other men were spiritual.
These three attitudes are reflected in the three
types of worship. A worship which is non-
mystical and controlled from above treats man
as natural. A worship which is partially mystical, recognising the presence of God Himself
in the Church Universal and in the Mass, apprehends man as both natural and spiritual. A
worship which is wholly mystical and organic
and controlled from within assumes that man
is spiritual.' *

VII

Some comments wait to be made on Dr.
Brinton's thesis. First, however, it should be

* ibid., p. 83.

made clear that he is careful not to claim these virtues for Quaker worship always and everywhere; he is setting out the ideal—yet an ideal which is frequently achieved. Nor does he pretend that his criticisms of Protestant worship will always and in every respect hold; but he does claim that the Friends' mode of worship is far better adapted to real worship (and, as an incidental consequence, to growth in the practical Christian life) than is the Protestant mode. Further, he thinks that the Protestant method implies in itself a failure fully to grasp the true purpose of a meeting for corporate worship— at least, so am I bound to conclude from his argument.

Much of his criticism of Puritan worship is thoroughly salutary, although I should say it applies far more cogently to what may be called its ' debased ' form (alas ! too common) than to its classical forms. He is on firm ground where he combats its tendency in practice to ethical subjectivism. And yet (and may it not be counted unto him for righteousness?) he himself, being a good Quaker, is in truth essentially Puritan in his ethical interest, and I cannot see that he is a whit less concerned than the Puritan for the subjective effects of worship. One of his strong claims for Quaker worship is that through it the worshipper finds peace and inward harmonization, and he is at pains to contend that the Friends' method has proved itself the most effective in hastening advance in moral insight and in making men and women more truly Christian in their outlook and in their relations with their fellows.

No one, whose acquaintance with this form of cult has been fortunate, will be disposed to deny the virtues of the Quaker Meeting. The Church would be the poorer without the Quaker contribution to her cult life. It may well be agreed that there would be a great advance if the Church Meetings of the Independents were thoroughly schooled in Quaker ways. Moreover, the value of silence in public worship is becoming more and more to be appreciated in different branches of the Church, and no doubt it is largely from the Friends that this has been learned. This does not, however, mean a growing approximation to Quaker practice. It is evident that to incorporate a period of silence into an otherwise directed Service, while it may involve borrowing something valuable from the Friends, in no way converts that Service into one of the Quaker type. In the latter everything proceeds out of the Silence; in the former the Silence is but an important stage in a directed process.

The Quaker comes seeking that ' inner creative

life which the Mystics know to be God '. Neither much speaking nor external activity is required. All self-assertion must be stilled, and the worshipper must subdue himself to quiet in order to hear God speaking. There is manifestly much truth in this, and truth to which perhaps the Free Churches especially need to attend. But the question must be asked, How does God make Himself heard in the silence? Modern Christians would be, I suppose, in general agreement that God is always and everywhere trying to speak to His children. Is silence and willingness to listen to the Divine all that is required in order that the child may hear God's voice and gradually grow to a rich knowledge of Him?

Let us suppose an Animist, a Polytheist, a Hindu, a Buddhist, a Mohammedan, a Jew, a Christian, and an Agnostic all going into silent meditation in order to receive intimations of the Divine. If they hear anything at all, will there be any kinship in what they hear, so that in comparing their experiences they would all recognize the lineaments of the same God in the intimations they each received? It is hard to believe it. Indeed, it is safe to hazard that the more frequently they recurred to this religious exercise the more firmly incompatible would the views of some of them become.

In going into the silence a man does not, and cannot, make his mind a *tabula rasa* on which the deity will print his message. God's power to communicate Himself to us is conditioned by our capacity to receive, and that in turn depends largely on the mental and spiritual environment in which we have been nurtured. There is nothing peculiar to religious knowledge in this; the same principle applies to our acquiring knowledge of the external world. 'To him that hath shall be given' is a law which is operative in the whole realm of knowledge. Two observers of an event in the physical world may so differ in what they bring to the apprehension of it that they disagree not merely in their interpretation of what they observe, but also in their very experience, so that in describing what they have seen they may appear to be speaking of two unrelated events, although that which was objectively 'given' was precisely the same for both.

Let us borrow an illustration used by the Revd. C. F. Russell in his Opening Address to the Thirteenth Conference of Modern Churchmen. He supposes an astronomer and a savage both observing an eclipse of the sun and perceiving the gradual obscuring of the solar disc and the dwindling of daylight. 'The one may know that the eclipse is caused by the passage of the moon between the sun and the earth, and the other may believe that it is due to the voracity of a supernatural dog dwelling in the sky.' 'Would it be true', asks Mr. Russell, 'to say that the actual experience of these two observers differed only in the way in which they explained it? Surely not. To say so would be to leave out of account all those emotional elements which play so large a part in our lives. The astronomer's attitude is one of intense interest, fascination, satisfaction; the savage's is one of surprise, consternation, dread. And it is to be noted further that in consequence of the existence of these emotional differences there is likely to be also a difference in regard to what objective facts are actually observed.' It is, indeed, possible enough that the savage will be convinced that he truly 'saw just beforehand in the sky the dog which was preparing to swallow the sun'.*

Now the Quakers are in origin a Christian sect. They came to their fellowship and to their mode of worship not only with the Christian Scriptures but with centuries of the Christian tradition, of thought and theology and ethics and practice, behind them. In relation to their apprehension of that Inner Light which

* *The Modern Churchman*, Vol. XVI., Nos. 6, 7, and 8, p. 271 f.

lighteth every man they were in the position rather of the astronomer than of the savage when these two observed the eclipse of the sun. Had they not the knowledge of the glory of God in the face of Jesus Christ wherewith to interpret the whisperings of the Holy Spirit in the Silence? Was it not a possession which increased their sensitiveness to the Divine?

'The worshipper', writes Dr. Brinton in a passage to which I have already referred, 'may have approached the Divine Presence at odds with himself. Passions clash with ideals, desire is at odds with duty or self-depreciation with pride. Through prayer, contrition and self-surrender all these are sacrificed on the invisible altar. In the silence a voice is heard like that which once spoke to the stormy waves of Galilee, " Peace be still ".' * We are moving here along a road familiar to all Christians. Where Christians meet to worship God their procedure, however much it may vary in detail, bears witness to the soul's demand for confession, repentance, and absolution before it can enter freely into the worshipful communion which it seeks. Certainly the speaking and hearing implied in this can be done in silence, but notice two things about the conditions of this silence if it is to achieve its end. First,

* Op. cit., p. 49.

it is not merely a silence of receptivity. The worshipper himself must speak, though he does not do so vocally, and possibly he may not even *frame words* mentally. Second, the silence can convey the divine message only if the essence of it has already been spoken, it may be in word, it may be in act or event. I do not mean that the listener can never hear anything new, that he can never awake to a new insight in advance of anything that has been seen by his fellow-men. If that were true, progress would be impossible. But I do mean that the new which comes in the silence can arise only out of that which has already been proclaimed openly and in his hearing. The silence itself never gave the Quaker the theology which his prayer, his contrition, his self-surrender, presuppose; and as for the message of peace which follows in the silence these acts, whence comes it? The answer is tolerably plain : it comes from the Holy Land, where it was proclaimed in a Person, and it has reached the worshipper through the mediation of innumerable witnesses, whose inner experiences assured them that they witnessed to the truth.

The silence of the Quaker Meeting is rich and fruitful according to the knowledge and insight of those who participate in it. Where (as I make no doubt happened at the beginning of the Movement and as has happened frequently since) the Meeting is for the most part composed of what, for brevity, we may call expert Christians, sure of their faith and zealous in the living of it, this method of worship is well adapted to reach very high levels. It starts from an advanced position, and, because of its freedom from externals and its consequent sole dependence on the quickening Spirit, the worshipper is expectant of moving on to loftier ranges and is not tempted to linger on the lower slopes, and his desire and expectancy are rewarded.

VIII

There are, however, two outstanding deficiencies in this mode of worship. (1) It is deficient in missionary power, and (2) it is not of itself conservative of the faith. These two shortcomings are, of course, related. In some respects it might be better to state them in the reverse order, for the missionary deficiency to some extent results from the lack of the conservative factor—but it matters little, and I find the order chosen more convenient. The first is, I think, more generally recognized, even by the Friends themselves. It is not infrequent for them to hold Sunday evening meetings especially designed for outsiders. These meetings take on a form scarcely distinguishable from the ordinary simple Nonconformist Service. Both the enquirer and the catechumen need instruction not only about the fundamental nature of the Christian gospel but also in the elements of worship and devotion, which latter must be taught by outward and vocal example even if it be held that for the advanced Christian they are better conducted in the silence, save where the Spirit moves the individual to utterance for the benefit of the common fellowship. The request of the disciples, ' Lord, teach us to pray ', was not an altogether foolish one.

Moreover—and this bears on the second shortcoming as well as the first—the normal Friends' Meeting for Worship is not essentially and inevitably a setting forth of the heart of the Christian religion, it is not a *speculum Christi* as are the Communion Services of other Christian bodies or their other ' mechanistic ' Services (as Dr. Brinton calls them) in varying degrees. I do not mean that a particular meeting may not be this, but it is not a characteristic function. This becomes obvious when you reflect that a Meeting ' in the life '—a Meeting rich in edification for the initiated—may be carried through in complete silence and with no outward action or sign. There is here no ' setting forth ' to the world at large, or such part of it as may come within distance of sight and hearing.

I believe that in this the Quaker cult lacks something necessary to the continued life of a religion. It is a main function of a cultus to conserve the essential values of the religion out of which it arises. To these it bears witness before the world and before the passing generations of the faithful. No doubt if it is to achieve this it must change with changing thought and outlook, but, if the religion is to survive, the changes must be true to the heart of that religion, and such as will make it clearer and not more obscure. To perform this function the cultus must, therefore, have some specific content, it must set forth something definite. The Quaker cultus has no specific content, unless it be the bare affirmation of the Inner Light—and there is nothing peculiarly Christian in that.

IX

So far as my limited observation goes, I should say that the besetting danger of Quaker Worship is that of falling into a vague, and often sentimental, mysticism which bears very little relation to Christianity at all. Dr. Brinton himself seems to regard as the highest form of worship a mysticism which, though it is not sentimental and though it has had protagonists in the Christian Church, seems to me to have nothing specifically Christian about it. He says that there is no mapped road to the experience out of which new life is born, but that the great mystics have much to tell us regarding the steps on the way. Let me quote him again. ' The first step which has been emphasised by many is a so-called " purgation ". The soul must be cleansed of its appetites, desires and interests in order that its whole world may be built up anew from the beginning. If God is to create a higher life the worshipper must bring the lower to abeyance. Most Eastern mystics and the classic mystics of Christendom admonish us that we must not seek God by thinking of any particular object or action, for this will arrest the soul on its flight to the Universal who transcends all that is particular. . . . The mystic does not seek God by discursive reason. His search is for Life. Reason divides, analyses, distinguishes. Life is synthetic; it unites the part with the whole through the irrational sacrifice of each for the other. The mystic may have sought God because of inner conflict which he could not overcome. The more he struggled

the more the conflict increased. Each of the
forces within him grew strong by combating an
opposing force. He solves his problem by
purgation, that is, by denying both forces which
were tugging at him; and, fixing his attention
on the one God who transcends finite distinctions, he sinks back, relaxed and effortless, into
the Everlasting arms. At the centre of Life
out of which all new life is reborn he finds
peace and harmony of soul which can mould
the chaotic flux of existence into forms like
Itself.' *

Dr. Brinton admits that this *via negativa* has
often been over-emphasized, and that, following
it, men have fled from the world and found
peace, and then have not taken the way back.
His favourite mystic consequently is Jacob
Boehme, ' who discovered how the negative
and positive ways could be combined ', solving
the problem ' by finding that he could go inward
on the negative way to the Heart of God and
then, passing through this Divine Centre, he
could return on the positive way back to
nature '.†

In Boehme's mystical terminology there are
two worlds, the Dark world, and the Light
world. The Dark world is what, I suppose, we
should call the world of the natural man, or

* Op. cit., p. 57 f.   † ibid., p. 60.

rather, it is the world of unharmonized nature, for Boehme is not thinking only of human life. It is a world of opposing and warring forces leading to ever increasing chaos, because these forces are strengthened by what opposes them. Nature has no power of itself to end the conflict. A solution is found only when through exhaustion it sinks back into the One Being out of whom it came. At the Unifying Centre of all things is found peace and harmony. Having achieved unification and harmonization at the heart of the Universe, Nature emerges into the Light world. The Light world is, according to Boehme, the Son, the goal of Nature, the incarnation of God the Father in the forms of Nature. ' What is true of nature ' (I am quoting Dr. Brinton's exposition) ' is also true of man. Man cannot of himself solve the conflict within himself. Therefore he goes inward to God, but he does not remain there. He wants peace, but he wants a peace incarnate in the world. He returns to the world bringing with him the Creative Love of God through which the Son is born in the soul. A new and harmonized life emerges because, to use the word of Paul, the Christ is " formed " within. Boehme believes that our religious life is a continual alternation between the negative and positive ways. We go inward to find God and outward to manifest His life in the world. And because God has already been made manifest what we find outwardly helps us as well as what we find inwardly. That which keeps true our sense of the direction of the goal is the perfect incarnation in Jesus Christ.' *

There is, on the face of it, a definite Christian factor in this mystical conception, and it may occur to the reader, therefore, that I was not justified in my suggestion that there is nothing specifically Christian about the mysticism which Dr. Brinton seems to advocate as the highest form of worship. Perhaps my words do require some qualification; and yet I think that they are in the main just. The Christian element in Boehme's mystical philosophy seems to be something imported into it from outside rather than something which belongs to its very core. Remove it, and I do not see that his philosophy would be essentially altered.

Much of this mysticism is, I admit, unintelligible to me. To talk of Nature in general sinking back, out of exhaustion, into the One Being from whom it came, and then emerging into the Light world, conveys no comprehensible meaning to me whatsoever. If the reference is to some future apocalyptic transfiguration of the Universe, then, perhaps, it may be followed in

* Op. cit., p. 61 f.

a vague way, but I do not think that is its intention—and even if it were it would belong to the realm of wholly *a priori* speculation, differing in no rational way from pure fantasy.

To describe the Light world into which Nature emerges as ' the Son ', ' the incarnation of God the Father in the forms of Nature ', appears to be borrowing Christian language and applying it to a concept which is not recognizably Christian; a Christian name is used, but it is a name and nothing more, having lost its Christian content and signification.

When he comes to deal with human experience, Boehme does, it is true, find a definite place for the historic Christ, but at most it is only a useful one, not a necessary one. The soul finds peace, not by reconciliation to a God who is revealed in Jesus Christ, but by a tired sinking back into the Unifying Centre of Being. There it awakes to the Creative Love of God, which gives birth to the Son in it (the soul). (Notice that ' the Son ' in this context is apparently no more than a name for the soul's new and harmonized life.) The Incarnation is ' helpful ', it would seem, because it enables the soul to keep its direction when it has turned outwards again from God. The historic Christ in no sense mediates God to man; He plays no part in the process of atonement. Peace and harmony, in short, salvation, is apparently achieved quite independently of Him and independently of that for which He stood. Historical Christianity is turned completely upside down. Instead of the Son revealing the Father to mankind, man by losing himself in God brings the Son to birth. The difference in terminology is also very significant. The Gospel speaks continually of the ' Father '; this religion is of the ' One Being ', of the Unifying Centre of all things.

I do not believe that this form of mysticism enshrines the heart of Christianity, and I have dwelt on it at some length because it seems to me that Quakerism is prone to fall into it largely because it expresses itself in a cult which has no specific content apart from the general affirmation of the Inner Light. And yet, of course, the Friends as a body are, up to date, very close to the fount of the Christian religion, and their devotion and loyalty to Jesus bear issue in an advanced ethical and social conscience.

The branches of the Church are remarkably interdependent in spite of their great divergences, and sometimes their mutual hostility. It is an interesting speculation how far the vitality of one ecclesiastical organization is dependent upon its absorption of a particular ' vitamin ' in which it is naturally deficient from one or more of its neighbours.

X

Let us turn to consider the distinction upon which Dr. Brinton lays so much stress between 'mechanistic' and 'organic' worship.

Protestant worship, we are given to understand, is 'mechanical' because it employs means to work on the worshippers from outside, and it is not just the spontaneous expression of a worshipping group which has become a living organism, as is the 'organic' worship of the Friends. The different items of a Protestant Service are devices to set the members of the congregation moving in a certain direction.

It will be readily allowed that there is a broad distinction between the Quaker method on the one hand and the somewhat varying Protestant methods on the other, but the language which Dr. Brinton uses to describe this distinction is, in my judgement, both inaccurate and misleading. Think, for instance, what happens in a service when a passage from the Bible is read (it may have been selected by the minister with a special line of thought in view or it may have been prescribed by those who drew up an official lectionary). What is the effect on an individual hearer? Does it move him in a particular direction, whether of feeling or action or both, regardless of his own judgement and will? If it does not (and palpably it does not), its effect is not a mechanical effect, and it only confuses thought to call it so. Again, in the sermon the preacher may appeal to the reason, the conscience, the emotions, and so on of his hearers, but in so doing he is not working on them mechanically. The relations subsisting between him and his congregation are personal relations. Doubtless they may be of widely varying degrees of intimacy, but the impress is always one of personality upon personality. It is not in the nature of personal relations to be mechanistic; mechanism and personality belong to two entirely different realms.

Though he does not, as far as I can recollect, use the term, it is evident that Dr. Brinton regards Protestant Services as coercive in intention.

We may agree that there are religious gatherings, especially those of a revivalist kind, against which this is a just criticism; but then, whatever names may be given to such, they are not Services of Worship. Worship and coercion do not consort together. Surely, however, it betokens a serious misapprehension of common Protestant thought and practice to suppose that services are treated as instruments for forcing people into particular ways of thinking and feeling and acting. Certainly this is a travesty of Protestant *theory*, which is thoroughly congregational in its view of what constitutes public worship. It is highly doubtful if there is any Protestant body which would deny that in that part of the service which represents the forthgoing of man to God the task of him who leads the worship is to express as adequately as possible the worshipping heart of the congregation, and not either simply to express his own feeling or to instruct the people in what they should think or feel. This may be affirmed equally of the churches which are accustomed to *ex tempore* prayer and of those which follow a fixed liturgy. The liturgy is not for instruction, but for expression, and it is intended to express (whether it achieves its purpose or not) the common prayer and praise in the manner most conformable to the common Christian will. Similarly, it would be generally recognized as the duty of the minister who conducts the prayers in his own words to strive truly to represent verbally the will of his assembled brethren in worship. That some fail in this difficult task, and that some are heedless to it, must alas! be admitted, but those who are true to the spirit of Protestant worship not only know what their task is, but also are at pains to accomplish it; and they are many.

Then there is that part of the service which

represents the outcoming of God to man. It is of the Christian faith that God hath spoken unto us in a Son, that the Word became flesh and dwelt among us. Protestants believe that the demonstration of the Word is a vital and necessary part of public Divine Service. It is our bounden duty to set forth God's Holy Word with all possible cogency. To attempt to do this by the exercise of coercion is, however, to defeat the end in view. It is only as the Word is received by the insight of the worshipper that it is of any real avail. The cogency which awakens insight is not coerciveness.

XI

There is a faith ' once for all delivered unto the saints ', but it is far too stupendous a faith to be at once and everywhere apprehensible in all its implications. There is always the possibility of ' more light ' and of ' the emergence of the new '. Knowledge, as we have seen, is not something which can be simply imposed from outside; its acquirement is conditioned by the receptive quality of the observer, which in turn is conditioned by the insights achieved through previous experience. The Christian religion is not static; it has power to progress, and to give birth to the new, because the heights and depths of it are immeasurable. The new which emerges is, however, the consequence of that which has already been given; it is involved in the given. Only by attention to the given can a man awake to fresh meaning in it. Hence the importance of setting forth continually the once for all given, out of which alone the new which is also true will come to light. The premiss from which this argument proceeds is, of course, one which a non-Christian would not be prepared to grant, but I believe it is an inevitable presupposition of the Christian religion, if there is anything essentially distinctive in the adjective ' Christian '.

XII

That the Society of Friends has in the past been ahead of other Christian bodies in sensitiveness to the social implications of the Christian faith may certainly be due in considerable measure to its habit of corporate listening in the silence, and it presents here a lesson which should be pondered by the churches of a different order. And yet conclusions may be drawn from this assertion which are not warranted. If priority of insight and practice can be demonstrated for this Society over against other Christian corporations as a whole, such priority is not so easily proved in respect to individuals and groups within those corporations. The larger and more all-embracing a group the harder it is to be in advance of its age in corporate witness. The ' weaker brethren ' are a constant brake on its progress. It is not, I venture to suggest, so much their form of worship as the quality of their membership and its restriction which is responsible for the Friends having been in the vanguard of social enlightenment. Their strength is also their weakness. They cannot afford to admit to the privileges of the Society the backward and spiritually immature in any marked numbers if they desire to act in a body as pioneers of the Christian conscience. But Christ's Church cannot hold herself aloof from any, however weak, foolish, or immature, who would be of her fellowship in learning of her Lord and in His service. There is an inestimable contribution which the Society of Friends has made, and is making, to the Church as a whole; there is also a task which the Church must perform, and which she could not if she adopted universally Quaker ways. The Society's special gift to the Church is dependent on its exclusiveness.

There is a logical relation between the constitution of the Society of Friends and its form of worship. The latter is well adapted to the high purposes of small groups of what, for short, we may call 'advanced Christians', but for those less mature and those not grounded in the fundaments of historical Christianity its deficiencies as a Christian cult become prominent. Let the boundaries of the Society be widely extended, and it may be predicted that, unless its method of worship were greatly modified, its distinctive Christian quality would soon vanish, and with it what leadership it possesses in Christian social ethics. A vague mystical theism and a 'natural' humanitarianism are not Christianity, and they are not sufficient for the salvation of the world. Yet, if the opinion of one outsider who has seen some little of Quaker meetings is worth anything, these are weaknesses to which a larger Quakerism, undisciplined in the Christian thought and traditions of centuries, is in danger of succumbing.

Chapter V

Sacrifice

I

WE have already formulated the first principle of worship, namely that the essential act of worship is the bringing of a gift. That it is an age-long principle is evident from the place which sacrifice takes in the history of worship. Dr. Anderson Scott, writing on worship from the Free Church standpoint, asks ' What is the constructive principle to which we must seek to give expression, in which our worship is to find coherence and meaning? ' To find the answer, he tells us, it is only necessary to examine the Old Testament. ' There we find, underlying all the allusions to worship and all the regulations for its performance, the basal principle that the condition of man's approach to God, the accepted vehicle of worship, is sacrifice.' *

We should not be prepared, perhaps, to regard that answer as decisive, if, on other grounds,

* C. Anderson Scott, *The Church: Its Worship and Sacraments, A Free Church Interpretation*, p. 49.

there were reasons to think that the Old Testament view should be superseded; but it is not on the ground of history alone that this view is justified, in so far as sacrifice implies gift. The latter proviso is important, because Robertson Smith argued, it may be remembered, that the predominant idea in ancient sacrifice was communion, and not gift. ' The leading idea in the animal sacrifices of the Semites . . . was not that of a gift made over to the god, but of an act of communion, in which the god and his worshippers unite by partaking together of the flesh and blood of a sacred victim.' *

The late Dr. Buchanan Gray has, however, shown that, whatever may have been the origin of Hebrew sacrifice, in historical times the idea of gift was never absent.†

Our reading of ancient literature probably disposes us to think of sacrifice in the first place as a means of placating the deity, of humouring him.

> There hecatombs of bulls, to Neptune slain,
> High-flaming please the monarch of the main.‡

Sacrifice is propitiatory : to appease an angry god, or to keep in a favourable mood one who

---

* *Religion of the Semites*, p. 209.
† Vid. Gray, *Sacrifice in the Old Testament*, passim.
‡ *Odyssey* III, ll. 178–9 (Pope, ll. 217–18).

at any time may become angry. This notion is,
of course, common and primitive. A good Old
Testament illustration of it is to be found in
the account, in I Sam. xxvi, of the interview
between Saul and David. David, conscious of
no offence, wonders why Saul pursues him.
Saul presumably has some reason. Perhaps
men have been slandering him to Saul, or
perhaps Yahweh is responsible. If it be men,
David says to Saul, let them be accursed, but
' if it be Yahweh that hath incited thee against
me, let him smell an offering ' (xxvi. 19).*
That is the way to placate a god into whose
disfavour you have fallen. Notice that here
the suggested sacrifice is purely propitiatory.
There is no thought of the expiation of sin.
David, in the story, is not thinking of sin; his
thought is simply that Yahweh may be angry
for some reason only known to himself, and the
thing to do with an angry god is to try to
placate him with a sacrifice.

But ancient sacrifice was not only, nor always,
propitiatory in intention. That is very clear
in Hebrew religion. Often its purpose was
expiatory. For example, this is obvious in the
message which the child Samuel received from
Yahweh concerning Eli : ' I have sworn unto
the house of Eli, that the iniquity of Eli's house

† Vid. Gray, op. cit., p. 83.

shall not be expiated with sacrifice nor offering for ever.'   (I Sam. iii. 14.)

But more prominent in Hebrew practice than either propitiatory or expiatory sacrifice is a third type, namely, that which Gray calls ' eucharistic ' sacrifice—sacrifice of a festal character.   He shows the eucharistic purpose in the majority of legends describing the foundation of famous sanctuaries and in the two human-sacrifice stories (Abram and Isaac—Jephthah and his daughter), and also in the great annual festivals (cf. Deut. xvi. 16).*   In the earlier periods of the history of Israel, he says, ' sacrifice was more often eucharistic than propitiatory, and it was more often offered with feelings of joy and security than in fear or contrition '.†

It is important that we should keep clearly in mind these three classes of sacrifice with their three distinctions of aim : propitiatory, expiatory, and eucharistic.   All of them are to be found in the history of Christian worship.   The last only—and that in a spiritual form—has a rightful place according to Protestant thought ; and it is urgently to be desired that it should take its rightful place in Protestant practice.

* Op. cit., pp. 90 ff.   † ibid., p. 95.

II

For us there is no legitimate place for sacrifice in the sense of the performance of a rite which will 'work on' God so that He may forgive us, be favourable to us, or whatever the purpose. This conception is to be found in the Roman Mass, for instance, in the 'Offertory' prayer, when the priest takes the paten with the Host, and, offering it up, says:

Suscipe, sancte Pater, omnipotens aeterne Deus, hanc immaculatam hostiam, quam ego indignus famulus tuus offero tibi Deo meo vivo et vero, pro innumerabilibus peccatis, et offensionibus, et negligentiis meis, et pro omnibus circumstantibus, sed et pro omnibus fidelibus christianis vivis atque defunctis: ut mihi, et illis proficiat ad salutem in vitam aeternam.

(' Accept, O holy Father, almighty and eternal God, this unspotted victim which I, thine unworthy servant, offer unto thee, my living and true God, for my innumerable sins, offences, and negligences, and for all here present; as also for all faithful Christians, both living and dead; that it may avail both me and them unto life everlasting.')

It is to be found, again, in the Canon of the Mass, for instance, in the prayer beginning Te igitur, clementissime Pater, or in this prayer following the priest's elevation of the chalice for adoration :

Unde et memores, Domine, nos servi tui, sed et plebs tua sancta, eiusdem Christi Filii tui Domini nostri tam beatae passionis, nec non et ab inferis resurrectionis, sed et in coelos gloriosae ascensionis : offerimus praeclarae maiestati tuae de tuis donis, ac datis, hostiam puram, hostiam sanctam, hostiam immaculatam, Panem sanctum vitae aeternae, et Calicem salutis perpetuae.

Supra quae propitio ac sereno vultu respicere digneris : et accepta habere dignatus es munera pueri tui iusti Abel, et sacrificium Patriarchae nostri Abrahae : et quod tibi obtulit summus sacerdos tuus Melchisedech, sanctum sacrificium, immaculatam hostiam. . . .

('Wherefore, O Lord, we thy servants, as also thy holy people, calling to mind the blessed passion of the same Christ thy Son our Lord, his resurrection from the dead, and glorious ascension into heaven, offer unto thy most excellent majesty, of thy gifts bestowed upon us, a pure victim, a holy victim, an unspotted victim, the holy Bread of eternal life, and Chalice of everlasting salvation.

Upon which vouchsafe to look with a propitious and serene countenance, and to accept them, as thou wast graciously pleased to accept the gifts of thy just servant Abel, and the sacrifice of our Patriarch Abraham, and that which thy high priest Melchizedech offered to thee, a holy sacrifice, an unspotted victim.')

That the Eucharist is to be understood in the way which these words imply is made plain by the Roman Church. In the canons of the Council of Trent it is described as ' verum et proprium sacrificium ' and as ' vere propitiatorium '. Moreover, in chapter 2 of the 22nd Session it is stated that it is necessary that the Christ, who sacrificed himself once on the altar of the Cross in a bloody manner, shall be sacrificed perpetually in the Mass in a bloodless way.*

If this kind of thought is involved in the concept of sacrifice, then Protestantism is fundamentally anti-sacrificial, for modern Protestantism can find no rightful place for sacrifice which is in any sense ' theurgic '. But sacrifice is a term of wider range than that. Dr. Will, providing a formula which will include the whole scale of varied sacrificial forms, defines Sacrifice as ' a sacred act whereby man presents an offering which costs him something and which

* Vid. *Conc. Trid.*, sess. xiii. cap. 3 ; sess. xxii. cap. 2.

is pleasing to God '.* The formula may be
open to criticism, but at all events it would be
perverse to deny that when a man at some cost
offers to God what is believed to be pleasing
to Him, then the act is an act of sacrifice. The
offering of the self in humble thanksgiving to
God comes within this category, and sacrifice,
therefore, is a word which quite properly belongs
to the vocabulary of Protestant worship.

In drawing attention to the theurgic conception of sacrifice in the Mass I would not be
understood to suggest that the Mass is devoid
of the highest elements of Christian worship.
' Elle est tout un monde religieux ', says Dr.
Will;† and we shall be wise to go on studying
it until we have learned to appreciate it, even
though no modification can make it ours.
Moreover, it is in accordance with true Catholic
piety that the congregation at Mass should give
itself up in whole-hearted, trustful self-com-
mittal to Christ. As an illustration, where
many illustrations could be cited, take the ' Akt
der Aufopferung ' given in a leaflet intended to
serve as a guide before communion to the
faithful in the diocese of Strasbourg : ' O my
Jesus, I sacrifice to thee my body and my mind
and all which I possess for thy sacred service '.‡

* Op. cit., Vol. I., p. 116.
† ibid., p. 98.   ‡ Quoted Will, ibid., p. 107.

Such an act made unreservedly and in truth is a spiritual sacrifice which belongs to the heart of worship. But even here, of course, the religious value of the sacrifice is conditioned by the purity and disinterestedness of the motive. If it be undertaken with the hope of compelling the Divine favour it really moves in the realm of the impersonal and magical, or, at all events, the impersonal and magical is mixed with the personal and religious. That, however, is a danger to which all rites are open, and it is certainly not peculiar to Catholicism. Has no Protestant ever felt that by going to church he has done something meritorious, something which, in however slight a degree, will dispose God's favour towards him? Many a pious Jew attends the synagogue Service, because in so doing he is participating in a rite ordained by God, the mere performance of which is well-pleasing to Him.

III

The sacrifice which is not theurgic in intention, and which is inseparable from the loftiest forms of religion, is spiritual and ethical. ' The real material of sacrifice ', writes Dr. Anderson Scott, ' is . . . just ourselves, our whole personalities, made over as an offering to God. That gives us the basal principle of public worship, even as the life of those who are so made over to God will be a life of personal worship such as is described by St. James.' *

This means that the act of Sacrifice becomes an act of PRAYER. It is removed out of the material, or quasi-material, into the wholly spiritual. The transformation finds inimitable expression in the 50th Psalm. Let me quote a passage of it from Dr. Moffatt's translation :

> I need no bullock from your farms,
>   no goat out of your herds ;
> for all the wild things of the wood are mine,
>   and cattle in their thousands on the hills ;
> every bird in the air I know,
>   I own all roaming creatures on the plains.
> If I were hungry, I would not tell you ;
>   for the whole earth is mine and all it holds.
> Do I eat flesh of bulls ?
>   Do I drink blood of goats ?
>
> No, offer to God thanks as a sacrifice,
>   and pay your vows to the Most High ;
> call to me in your hour of need,
>   then I will rescue you, and you shall honour me.
>
>   (Ps. l. 9–15.)

---

* Op. cit., p. 52. The reference is clearly to James i. 27 : Pure θρησκεία (i.e., religion in its external aspect, worship) and undefiled before our God and Father is this, to visit the fatherless and widows in their affliction, and to keep himself unspotted from the world.

And this is the sacrifice which the author of the Epistle to the Hebrews calls upon his readers to make. ' Through him [Jesus] then let us offer up a sacrifice of praise to God continually, that is, the fruit of lips which make confession to his name.' (Heb. xiii. 15.) It is the spiritual sacrifice which a spiritual and personal religion demands.

> Du willst ein Opfer haben,
> hier bring'ich meine Gaben :
> mein Weihrauch und mein Widder
> sind mein Gebet und Lieder.*

So sings the great Lutheran hymn-writer Paul Gerhardt. It is a simple thought, simply put, but it touches the centre of worship. Is it a thought prominent in the mind of the modern Nonconformist when he has taken his place in chapel for a service? With some, perhaps; but with the majority, I gravely doubt it. We have forgotten what a service is for.

---

* Quoted Will, op. cit., Vol. I., p. 114. We might render freely :

> Thou willest an offering.
> My little gift I bring :
> For smoke of sacrifice
> My prayer and praise suffice.

Sacrifice

It is probable that we have here one outstanding reason for the feebleness of church attendance in these days. That, at all events, is the opinion of M. le Pasteur A.-N. Bertrand in regard to French Protestantism. Let me quote an interesting passage of his—a passage which Free Churchmen in this country might well ponder.

He begins by contrasting the state of affairs amongst Catholics and Protestants. The indifference of Protestants is displayed in a way opposite to that of Catholics. It shows itself, not as a rule by a contempt of Protestantism, but by abstention from public worship. While there is a vast number of practising Catholics who have no sympathy with either the government or the ideal of the Church, we Protestants, on the contrary, have a great number of sympathizers who are proud to call themselves Protestants, but who do not attend our services. We are not burdened by adherents who dislike us, but we are abandoned by people who like us. Why, asks M. Bertrand, do they not come to Worship? (Pourquoi ne viennent-ils pas au culte?) And this is his answer: Parce qu'ils n'y trouvent pas, ou ne savent pas y trouver UN CULTE. (Because they do not find there,

or do not know how to find there, DIVINE
WORSHIP.) The majority, he continues, are
poisoned by excessive fondness for the sermon,
and a great number of regular church-goers
with them. (La plupart sont intoxiqués par
la manie du sermon, et nombre de non-indiff-
érents avec eux.) They come to a *preaching*
(Ils vont *au prêche*); and since the preaching
does not always interest them, they do not
come any more (et comme le prêche ne les
intéresse pas toujours, ils n'y vont plus). But
what about the SERVICE? (Mais LE CULTE?)
Do you believe, he asks, that they would give
it up in like manner if they had found it?
(Croyez-vous qu'ils l'abandonneraient de même
s'ils l'avaient trouvé?) Même avec la piété la
plus robuste, on peut se fatiguer des sermons;
c'est un malheur qui arrive. Mais on ne se fatigue
pas d'adorer Dieu. (Even the strongest piety
may weary of sermons—it is a misfortune
which happens—but one does not weary of
worshipping God.)*

M. Bertrand urges that we should give due
weight to the simple and obvious principle that
' un culte est un culte ',† *i.e.* that a Service is
a *Service*, that Divine Worship is Divine *Worship*.

* Vid. the paper by A.-N. Bertrand entitled ' L'adoration
dans le culte protestant ' in *L'église*, p. 68 f.

† Vid. op. cit., p. 64.

There is much need that we should, and that we should bear in mind that the act of worship implies, first and foremost, *giving*, whatever blessings of receiving may be implied also. A Service is an occasion for offering sacrifice.

v

We may fittingly close this discussion with another quotation from Buchanan Gray's lectures on the Hebrew theory of sacrifice, partly because it will remind us of the development of thought in relation to sacrifice, and partly because it will serve as a link to the theme of the next chapter. It is as follows.

' It is not in my judgement of great moment for an understanding of historical Hebrew and Jewish religion and their contribution to Christian thought to determine whether Jewish sacrifice originated in the idea of communion or the idea of gifts to God, nor to discuss whether at various periods the type of sacrifice which may with most probability be most closely related to an original conception of communion is dominant or not. The truth is whatever is the root idea, if either is so exclusively, that root idea belongs to a grossly material view of religion and of man's relation to God. It was just as little possible for a growingly ethical and spiritual religion to revert to the earliest idea of communion as to the earliest idea of gift; both alike run back to a materialistic conception of God or the God, to the thought that the gods like men eat and drink. I have argued that the conception of sacrifices as gifts to God was vital, perhaps at its most vital, in the first century; but nothing could be more misleading than to say that the religion had moved away from the early conception of sacrifice as communion to a later conception of sacrifice as propitiatory gift. This would be to represent it as a descent. On the other hand the real movement is of course upward. The belief that God receives material gifts from man for his own use, the religion abandons; but its progress was not merely negative. It rises to the conception that there is a gift which man can make to God, a gift of something that is his own and that God desires to receive; man can give himself; his will is his own, he can make it his present to God. But this is also to say that through the idea of gift spiritualized the idea of communion is reached—not the material communion of primitive thought; but communion of spirit. Thus in reaching this point, even in the realm of sacrificial thought, the religion has travelled the whole way from a

Sacrifice

prehistoric, material starting-point through stages where the material still exercises its influence, particularly in maintaining a ritual of which the original meaning had been outgrown, to a completely spiritual goal.' *

* Gray, op. cit., p. 54.

I

WE have seen that the essential act of worship is an act of sacrifice, and that the highest form of sacrifice is an act of prayer. Prayer is not a one-sided activity; it is a commerce between the human spirit and the Divine Father of our spirits, and it thus presupposes communion. Communion with God, then, is the end to which worship moves. This remains true even though the pure spirit of worship does not, I think, concern itself with a good to be achieved; it simply worships, and in so doing it engages in an activity which is in itself good and satisfying, an activity which is not felt to be a means to something more. And yet, perhaps just because it is not consciously sought as a selfish acquisition, that something more is added, giving a supremacy to the act in human experience.

The final end of worship is a deepening of communion. I say ' deepening ' because, when we reflect on it, we see that worship itself does,

and must, spring out of communion. It is
experience of Divine grace which moves to
worship in the first instance; it is not we who
take the initiative, but God; we love him,
because he first loved us; our offering of ourselves in thankful dedication is a response, not
a tentative overture. To use the language of
the schools, communion with God is, therefore,
not only the ' final cause ' of worship, it is also
the ' efficient cause.' *

This truth that communion is the beginning
and the end of worship has an important bearing on the form proper to a Service. It means
that the structure should be such as best to
facilitate both *expression* and *creation*, the
expression of the religious consciousness of the
group, and the creation of a deeper apprehension of God. Schleiermacher held that
only expressive action (*darstellendes Handeln*)
is legitimate, that the sole purpose of a service
of worship should be to set forth the movement
of spirit which animates the religious group,
and that it is no part of a service to create
anything, and consequently there is no place
for *wirksames Handeln*.† His view represents
a wholesome reaction both against the obsessive
determination to instruct (which, incidentally,

* Cf. Will, op. cit., Vol. I., p. 64.
† Vid. Will, ibid.

is a major disease of modern English Non-conformity) and also against the formalism which works *per opus operatum*, but it would seem needlessly to impoverish the value which a service may possess.

II

Prayer is the pervading characteristic of Protestant worship. The question arises, In what relation does the prayer of an organized service stand to private, individual prayer?

Let us think for a moment of private prayer.

'When ye pray, ye shall not be as the hypocrites : for they love to stand and pray in the synagogues and in the corners of the streets, that they may be seen of men. Verily I say unto you, They have received their reward. But thou, when thou prayest, enter into thine inner chamber, and having shut thy door, pray to thy Father which is in secret, and thy Father which seeth in secret shall recompense thee. And in praying use not vain repetitions, as the Gentiles do : for they think that they shall be heard for their much speaking. Be not therefore like unto them : for your Father knoweth what things ye have need of, before ye ask him.   After this manner therefore pray ye : Our Father . . .' *

I do not see how it is possible to read the Gospels without coming to the conclusion that for the Lord Jesus prayer was in essence simple, genuine converse with God; and that surely should be regulative of our Christian conception of prayer. Yet the principle runs counter to a great mass of teaching on prayer, and it runs counter to the practice of many who are commonly regarded as experts in the devotional life. Who would ever suppose from a study of the Gospels that the true end of prayer is self-obliteration in mystical union with God? In the prayer-world of the Gospels distances are kept. That is not to 'say that *barriers* are maintained, but rather that there is preserved that mutual respect which, in human relationships, is a condition of the richest and most intimate unity of two personalities. The principle may be stated succinctly by saying that the end of prayer is communion, not union.

The relation which should obtain between God and man in prayer is most truly figured, as it was figured by Jesus, as that obtaining between father and child. That this should be the Christian view would seem plain enough, and yet how far it is from being regarded as

* Matt. vi. 5 ff.

obvious may be judged from the following satisfactory passage in Dr. Grensted's Bampton Lectures. ' If we venture ', he says, ' to suggest that what is called vocal prayer, such prayer, clothed in direct and consciously chosen words, as most nearly resembles the speech of man with man, such prayer as any child, scholar, or saint may utter when he will, is the highest prayer of all and not merely an elementary stage of some more honourable or more effective way, we shall be speaking contrary to all received religious opinion, but, I think, very comfortably to simple and sincere souls.' * There is, I should say, a touch of exaggeration in this ' all received religious opinion ', but it is only exaggeration, not fundamental misrepresentation. In so far as it is true, it goes to show how far removed is ' received religious opinion ' from the opinion of Jesus Christ as we can gather it from our records of his teaching and practice.

This private prayer which is the converse of the individual soul with God is naturally spontaneous and direct, regardless of form and style, of grammar, or of the right word in the right place. It speaks out of the abundance of the heart, and its range is the whole range of the heart's interests, bounded only by the limitation implied in St. Augustine's famous dictum :

* *Psychology and God*, p. 89.

*hoc licet orare, quod licet desiderare.** I do not know that the sense of what it means can be better conveyed than in the following words of Sir Wilfred Grenfell. 'The privilege of prayer to me is one of the most cherished possessions, because faith and experience alike convince me that God Himself sees and answers, and His answers I never venture to criticize. It is only my part to ask. . . . In the quiet of home, in the heat of life and strife, in the face of death, the privilege of speech with God is inestimable. I value it more because it calls for nothing that the wayfaring man, though a fool, cannot give— that is, the simplest expression to his simplest desire. When I can neither see, nor hear, nor speak, still I can pray so that God can hear. When I finally pass through the valley of the shadow of death, I expect to pass through it in conversation with Him.' †

How can private prayer become formalized and generalized into public prayer without losing all, or nearly all, its vitality? What function can public prayer fulfil which is not far better fulfilled by the individual in private? Is not public prayer simply a survival from the days

* *Ep. ad Prob.* 130, 12.
† Quoted by R. H. Coates, *The Realm of Prayer*, Appendix C, p. 290, from H. E. Fosdick, *The Meaning of Prayer*, pp. 39, 40.

when the group and not the individual was regarded as the religious unit? Questions of this tenor arise in the minds of most thoughtful religious people, some of whom are unhesitating in an answer adverse to public prayer. They arise largely, I think, because of the contrast which is actually felt between the warm intimacy of private prayer and the colder abstractions of public prayer. That corporate services have a most important function to fulfil we have already seen, and we have seen also that the pervading characteristic of the most spiritual worship is prayer. What conclusion are we to draw? Is it that ideally public prayer should copy private prayer in its intimacy, its detail, its particularity, as closely as possible, so that it may be held to be exemplified at its highest when it most nearly approximates to private prayer?

The answer must be a definite, No. The difference in the conditions of private and public prayer demands a difference in the manner of them. Public prayer cannot be approximated to private prayer without compromising its value. The individuals composing a group are never so identical in temperament, in thought, in experience, that single expression can be given to the will of each in all its fullness and its manifold particularity.

The truth is that the participation of the

individual in corporate worship requires devotional self-denial, if he be one of a rich devotional life, and yet this self-denial, while in some respects and for the time a restriction, issues in an enlargement of spirit and a richer personal devotional life. Private devotion and public worship are not alternatives, the latter for the weaker brethren, the former for the stronger. They are both necessary to the fullest and most blessed family life which is life in the Kingdom of God. If they are both as they should be, the one reacts upon the other : the quality of the private communion with God qualifies the gift which the worshipper brings to share with the community, the wider range of vision of the community sends the worshipper back to more far-reaching communion in the privacy of his heart with the Father of all.

But when that has been said, the objection may still be pressed by some that the necessary formalities, the generalities, the preparedness, of public prayer are hardly to be reconciled with the spontaneous freedom of the filial relationship enjoyed by the individual in his or her daily life. Will there not inevitably be some unreality about them?

A sufficient answer to this objection is, I suppose, that, however difficult the reconciliation may be in theory, the experience of those

to whom corporate worship is precious gives
the lie to the charge of unreality. The objection
is academic, which is as much as to say that it
contains a fallacy, whether or not that fallacy
is easy to detect.

The fallacy resides, I believe, in an illegitimate
use of an analogy, the analogy of the relation
between earthly child and father employed to
figure what should be the relation of man to God
in prayer. This is the most adequate available;
but it must be remembered that the terms
' Father ' and ' child ' thus used are metaphors,
and, as Dr. Wheeler Robinson has wisely said,
' we cannot build arguments on the elaboration
of a metaphor, as theology has too often done '.*

That these metaphors can easily be elaborated
to the extent of becoming false is plain when we
consider that an earthly child speaks to his
earthly father in order to convey information of
some sort—it may be about his interests, his
feelings, his thoughts, his perplexities, and so
on—information which frequently the father
would not possess if the child did not speak.
But we cannot tell God what He does not know
already. ' Your Father knoweth . . . before
ye ask him.' As the Archbishop of York has
said,† ' we never ' (he means, of course, never

* *The Christian Experience of the Holy Spirit*, p. 280.
† In a letter to *The Times*, Jan. 5, 1932.

if we are intelligent) ' use words in prayer in order to inform the Divine Mind, but always and only in order to fix our own thoughts '.

This surely is an incontrovertible principle, and it has a powerful bearing on the ' legitimacy ' of the language of public worship. It also has implications not always realized in regard to the frame of mind in which a man may rightly approach God in private prayer. Forgetting it, some whose prayer-life is active and beneficent seem to treat God much as if He were the kindly and paternal occupier of the flat upstairs. Such an attitude involves much personal impoverishment to them, however true it may be that their practical religion is far more vital than that of many whose theoretical conception of God is less trivial and unworthy. The growth of a truly religious man's personality is conditioned by the greatness of his conception of the Eternal and Living God. I think we can see, therefore, that the more formal, and, if you like, more ' distant ' ways of public worship may serve as a salutary corrective to a false intimacy in private prayer by conveying a sense of the Divine ' otherness ' which enhances the glory of His gracious Fatherhood.

III

The paradox of 'nearness' and 'distance' which meets us in the Bible and in later Christian literature does not point to a muddle-headed inability to be rid of outworn conceptions, but rather bears witness to a truth of life which can be expressed only by images which are superficially irreconcilable. Nowhere does it stand out more clearly than in Jesus himself. Who was ever more approachable than he? Jesus remote? The children, the sick, the sinful, the needy, knew better. In his presence artificial barriers separating person from person are removed. There was a direct simplicity about his contact with men and women and children, a naturalness, an intimacy of mind and spirit. Yet, on the other hand, will it be denied that there is also a sense in which he was remote as no other man has ever been? Mark has a touch in his description of that last journey up to Jerusalem which sets in relief a quality in Him which is discernible throughout the Gospel narrative. 'And they were in the way, going up to Jerusalem; and Jesus was going before them : and they were amazed; * and they that followed were afraid.' † (x. 32). In spite of all

* ἐθαμβοῦντο.   † ἐφοβοῦντο.

our rationalisms we cannot for long remain blind to the *mysterium Christi*. It is his very 'distance' which makes his 'nearness' so unspeakably wonderful. Moreover, directly we lose the reverence which is aware of the 'distance', we lose in proportion the 'nearness', for what is then felt as near is not the Lord Jesus (whom to know is to hold in utmost reverence) but a substitute of our own poor imagination, or at most a faint and distorted reflexion of Him.

This paradox of 'nearness' and 'distance' applies to God the Father no less.

'In the year that king Uzziah died I saw the Lord sitting upon a throne, high and lifted up, and his train filled the temple. Above him stood the seraphim: each one had six wings; with twain he covered his face, and with twain he covered his feet, and with twain he did fly. And one cried unto another, and said, Holy, holy, holy, is the LORD of hosts: the whole earth is full of his glory. And the foundations of the thresholds were moved at the voice of him that cried, and the house was filled with smoke. Then said I, Woe is me! for I am undone; because I am a man of unclean lips, and I dwell in the midst of a people of unclean lips: for mine eyes have seen the King, the LORD of hosts.' (Isaiah vi. 1–5.)

Treated as the poetry which it is, is this alien to genuine Christianity?

Now let us set beside it something very different.

" I don't think I ever had a bedside manner, nor wore felt slippers . . . but I did try to tidy myself when I wanted to come into the presence of God. Not *always*, because there were times when I wanted God horribly, as you want food when you are starving, or help when you are drowning or in a fire; and when you feel like that you forget all the proprieties. And when I come to think of it, it was often when I wanted Him so much that I forgot the proper ways of coming to Him that I seemed to find Him best. . . . And there were times when in His love and in His pity *He* found *me*, unexpectedly, and made me conscious of His presence in His healing and strengthening power. . . . But until about three years ago I used to think the right thing was to tidy up, and be grave and prepared in my mind. . . . But now it is different. What is the difference, you say? Well, I'm not quite sure, but I think it is something like this. All that time the world was really a school. And though I called God *Father*, I really thought of Him as a lot of other things first—Schoolmaster, King, Lord Almighty, and so on; and afterwards, or with an effort, I remembered He was

Father, though even then He was sometimes a long way off. It had never really got down into my mind that He was *my* Father. And now it is different. I'm not at school; I've come home. It is my Father's house, and it's awfully jolly to live at home with Him there *always*. So why shouldn't I go in and out freely? . . . And if I hum on the stairs, don't you understand the joy of being free? " *

Whatever criticisms we may feel inclined to make on what is contained in this passage we shall probably agree that the writer is describing a conversion in her religious life which marked an enormous advance in Christian understanding and in spiritual vitality. Later on she uses this device of letters to Parson John to tell what amazing new power and life came to her from this revolution in her attitude towards God. A metaphor—a metaphor constantly on the lips of the Lord himself—suddenly for her accomplished its work and gave her access to a newer, truer, richer, more real world; but a metaphor, as has been said already, must not be elaborated too far, and even here we see evidence of the danger of over-elaboration. Such teaching requires to be balanced by an Isaianic insight into the holiness of God.

* *God in Everything*—Letters of Miriam Gray, pp. 6–7 (Epworth Press).

Take the statement ' it's awfully jolly to live
at home with Him ', and place over against it
the lines of Thomas Binney :

> Eternal Light ! Eternal Light !
> How pure the soul must be,
> When, placed within Thy searching sight,
> It shrinks not, but with calm delight
> Can live and look on Thee !

Which rings truer to real religion ? My first
impulse is to say unhesitatingly the latter; but
reflexion brings me to the view that the question
does not admit of an answer one way or the
other, provided one does not look too much at
the crudity of expression of the former, but
rather gathers from the context what the author
is trying to express. If I read them aright, both
ring true to real religion, and the seemingly
incompatible views to which Miriam Gray and
Thomas Binney give expression in fact represent
complementary truths, both of which the profoundest religion must assimilate. Miriam Gray
is straining to awaken her readers to the nearness, the actuality, of God—to make them
realize what a saving revolution it means to
accept in simplicity the teaching of Jesus about
the Fatherhood of God. Binney's hymn is the
writing of a man sensitive to the stupendous
meaning for which the name GOD stands. The
one is bearing witness to the gracious and

inescapable ' nearness ', the other to the awe-
some and immeasurable ' distance '. Both
represent the truth, and a failure to recognize
either of these facets of the truth inevitably
results in the stunting of the spiritual life.

IV

In public worship what is the unit which
worships?—the individual or the group? If the
Protestant has to answer one or the other I
believe he will be nearer the truth by saying the
group rather than the individual. The obligation to *corporate* worship arises out of the
essentially *social nature* of Christianity and out
of the privilege of Christian sharing. A service
should be a great corporate act.

There is, of course, an obvious sense in which
even in corporate prayer it is the individual who
is the unit, but it is the individual in a special
relation, and it is this which makes it perhaps
truer to say that it is the group which is the unit.
In true corporate prayer the individuals composing the praying group are in a relation to one
another of mutual and voluntary subordination.
They give of their individuality to a common
end, so that the contributions of each and all
may be synthetized into a wider unit, to the
enrichment of all concerned.

Both Catholic and Protestant are familiar with corporate prayer in public worship, but they differ in emphasis about the body or collectivity which worships. For the Protestant (unless he be inveterately individualistic) the praying unit is the particular congregation of believers gathered together for a particular Service. This congregation represents the Church Universal at the given time in the given place, and, if it has a proper sense of the Church, it is conscious of the great cloud of witnesses, and its worship is wonderfully enhanced by its feeling of unity with the unseen Church militant throughout the world and with the unseen Church triumphant. The emphasis is, however, on the visible fellowship embodying the great Church at the particular time and the particular place. For the Catholic, on the other hand, the praying unit is the Catholic Church acting through its accredited representative the priest, and the actual congregation is of secondary importance (which is not the same as to say that it is regarded by Catholics as of no importance).*

* Cf. Will, op. cit., Vol. I., p. 224 f. Cf. also Heiler, *Prayer*, E.T., p. 341 f. : ' Not a few of the prayers in the Mass which sound on the lips of the priest are indeed the same as those with which the primitive Church gave thanks and offered supplications. But the liturgical prayer of the Mass is no longer common prayer. . . . The

Communion

The distinct emphases will probably always remain between the two, but there are signs—and they are welcome signs—that each is learning to see that there is value in the emphasis of the other, and possibly to modify that emphasis in the light of what he sees. There is a movement in the Roman Church, notably among the Benedictines, towards fostering the sense of communion between the members of the congregation assembled at Mass, and also towards emphasizing the spiritual character of the Church regarded as the *corpus Christi mysticum* rather than as an hierarchic institution.* Protestantism, in its turn, is becoming less local in its thought, and has a growing sense of the great Church. This applies to the English Free Churches no less than to the Anglican Church and the national Churches abroad. It is an interesting speculation how far the Oxford Movement is responsible for this change in Protestantism.

V

As we are concerned with public worship chiefly from the Protestant angle, we shall do well to pay special attention to the dangers to

prayer of the people present at the Mass is not *common* but *individual* prayer.'   * Cf. Will, ibid.

which Protestant practice is especially open. The Protestant stress on the congregation—the concrete fellowship—is thoroughly sound when it is made with the right understanding, but it ceases to be sound when it is made, consciously or unconsciously, solely in the interests of psychological effects. A desire for the large congregation may possess little or no spiritual quality and be simply a morbid craving for emotional stimulus; and sometimes a minister, despondent at the meagre apparent results of his ministry, entertains it because of the quicker and more immediately visible returns which follow on the raising of the emotional temperature by a crowd.

On this matter Professor W. L. Sperry has some very wise words.

' Current manuals on church method ', he says, ' are apt to contain interesting and suggestive advice as to the judicious application of the laws of crowd psychology to the salvation of souls. The great preachers and revivalists of the past undoubtedly availed themselves of these laws, which operated reliably even though they had not been suspected or formulated. Perhaps we may wink at the times of that ignorance. But the case is otherwise to-day. Frank resort to devices suggested by modern psychology, whether of the unconscious or of the herd, does not make for moral confidence in a service of worship which is supposedly addressed to God. They suggest a back-stage apparatus for the manipulation of souls which is too mechanical. Real religion is always reluctant to manipulate souls precisely because it cares so much for souls. Once let a man suspect that his soul has been man-handled for his own good under the guise of the worship of God, he being unconscious at the time of what is being done to him, and he reacts against the whole transaction. The elder theology was on morally safer ground when it held that grace is the gift and work of God.' *

After indicating that the spread of popular knowledge of psychology will tend to make men on their guard against the common characteristics of crowd behaviour (so that in self-defence they will freeze instead of melt when they suspect that anything is done to raise the temperature), Professor Sperry continues :

' The facts with which the social psychologist deals will always be present in the great congregation. The psychologist will find in a service of public worship much that interests him and confirms him in his conclusions. But a service of worship cannot be translated into the direct manipulation of men by men and keep its integrity. So conceived and conducted it ceases

* *Reality in Worship*, p. 170.

to be worship and becomes a clinic in morality. The secret of the power and efficacy of a service of worship lies in men's confidence in its absolute integrity. Its eye must be single for God.' *

The social experience which is supremely valuable in corporate worship is one which does not come within the sphere of the laws of crowd psychology, for the simple reason that the bodily presence of even a modest number is not necessary to it. 'Our most profoundly social experiences', says Professor Sperry, 'are strangely independent of the crowd. A genuinely social experience of Christianity is a vision of the church triumphant in heaven far more than the sum of the sensations stirred by the church militant on earth. You do not have to sit in a crowded pew, or in a group circle to have a deeply social experience of religion. . . . The social confirmation which a church adds to private experience seems to be a matter standing quite free of the actuality of other fellow worshipers at any given time.' †

That is perfectly true in its bearing on the irrelevancy of crowd psychology. We must remember, however, that to affirm that the actual presence of fellow-worshippers is not necessary to a rich social experience is not to affirm that the presence of fellow-worshippers is

* *Reality in Worship*, p. 171.   † ibid., p. 174.

never of any importance. That would be absurd. What should be clear is that the social and religious value of participation in a worshipping group is not to be looked for in the psychological effects which a herd *quâ* herd produces. The full social value which is religious is to be found as much in the company of the two or three believers as it may be in a company of such numbers as would constitute a crowd from the psychologist's point of view.

VI

It is in relation to the truly corporate prayer of the visible group that I believe the Free Churches have a distinctive and valuable contribution to make to Christian public worship, although I do not think their services as commonly conducted to-day are very well adapted to making that contribution. The distinctive practice that I have in mind is that the prayers will be so uttered and of such a nature that it is possible, and is the normal rule, for the congregation to pray them unitedly; in short, the congregation will be throughout united in direction of thought and will. It is not possible, nor for that matter would it be desirable, for there to be absolute identity of thought and feeling. Much of the richness of the corporate act will come from the variety of contribution to it which the individual members of the congregation bring, but it will be a really corporate act in that the words audibly used will be prayed by the congregation as a whole. To some, I fancy, this principle will sound such a platitude as scarcely to be in need of mention; but it is in fact far from being a platitude, for it is contrary alike to ' Catholic ' theory and to much Protestant theory and practice.

The author (whose identity is not, and probably is not intended to be, hidden by his anonymity) of ' The Devotional Companion ' to ' The Order of Divine Service ' used at the King's Weigh House Church states the prevalent view of what we may call for convenience the liturgical churches with his usual clarity. ' Liturgical prayer ', he says, ' . . . while a genuine offering of prayer, often composed by saintly minds and religious geniuses, is only meant to provide a ground or background of prayer, from which we rise to spontaneous private utterance, or from which, by a still higher flight, we pass beyond the realm of words, thoughts and even feelings, and with a blank and naked intent stretch our souls out in worship and desire towards God.' *

A similar claim is sometimes made for free or

* *The Devotional Companion*, p. 30.

ex tempore prayer in public worship, and for my part I agree that only on the theory which is identical with that of liturgical usage can much *ex tempore* prayer in its classical and traditional form be justified. Let me quote a passage where the claim is made. It occurs in a dialogue, published in 1856, by Thomas Binney, entitled ' Are Dissenters to have a Liturgy? ' The discussion purports to take place in the Reading Room of the Milton Hall and Club, and the person of the dialogue whom I am about to quote is an advocate of *ex tempore* prayer.

' He that teaches religion must *have* religion ;— that, you know, is the essential condition to a man's being a minister. In the same way, he that has to lead the prayers of others must be filled with the spirit of prayer himself, whether he pray with a Liturgy or without one. I will not deny that I have sometimes enjoyed the Liturgical service of the Church of England ; but I have also, I must affirm, been as much disturbed by the way in which that Liturgy has been read, as ever I was with the worst specimens of extemporary prayer. But besides this, I object to your *theory* of public prayer. It is, I think, imperfect and unspiritual. I don't admit that the only idea of public devotion is that of the people *actually praying*,—offering up, *in words*, as their own, every petition presented to God. There is that *spirit* of prayer of which you speak,—a spirit which is not always *brought* to the house of God, even by the best and holiest of men. Public prayer is to *excite* this as well as to express it, or to aid its expression. Now, I do maintain that where the minister is what he ought to be, there is more likelihood of his *exciting* devotion by free prayer than by the use of familiar forms, however unexceptionable and excellent in themselves. I have heard prayers which have gradually kindled, elevated, and enlarged the souls of the wrapt yet subdued people, by their solemnity and richness, in a way which was utterly indescribable, but which no Liturgy that was ever framed could possibly effect! The heart has been touched and softened; all sorts of emotion called forth; the truths of the common faith, implied in every sentence, have been brought before the mind with luminous clearness, and made to act with a penetrating power; penitence, faith, hope, joy, with all other corresponding sentiments, have been evoked and sustained; the invisible has been revealed; the world has disappeared; the presence of " the Comforter " has seemed a consciously felt reality! Such seasons are " times of refreshing from the presence of the Lord ", when the assembled Church feels " the powers of the

world to come ". Every man with the slightest
spark of Christian life in him feels bettered,
enriched, purified, exalted;—he is humbler,
stronger;—more loving, more holy, more joyous;
—" filled ", by a Divine blessedness, " with ",
or " unto ", " all the fulness of God ! " Yet,
with all this, few or none might be conscious of
directly offering up prayer,—offering, I mean,
the words of any one of the petitions uttered,—or
of *literally* uniting in, by actually repeating, what
they heard of adoration, contrition, confidence,
or joy. *You* would say that they did not pray,
or that they did not join in prayer with the
minister and with each other,—that they only
listened to another praying. *I* say that *their
whole spiritual nature prayed*; their souls were
a living sacrifice; they themselves were a
petition,—presenting and constituting such a
prayer as you read of when it is said, " The
Spirit maketh intercession in us " in a manner
that " cannot be uttered ".' *

These citations raise the question of free
versus liturgical prayer. It is a question which
demands careful consideration, but a preliminary
question has to be answered before discussion of
it can be profitable.

The issue is this : Are the uttered prayers in a

* *Baird on Liturgies* with an Introduction and Appendix
by Thomas Binney, pp. 308–310.

service intended to be followed and prayed, if not word for word, at any rate in their general sense and direction? Or are they intended primarily as a stimulus to individual prayer—either by exciting the spirit of devotion generally, or by providing a great number of stimuli, one or more of which will find a response in the individual and set him off on a special line of devotion of his own? The latter view has the support of Orthodox Eastern theory and practice, Roman theory and practice, and perhaps increasingly of Anglican too; it is also supported by the practice, and to some extent by the theory (in so far as individuals theorize on the subject), of the Evangelical Free Churches.

It may be said that it is the experience of many that the prayers of a service have served them in all these ways, and that each way has its value. That doubtless is true; but the issue is nevertheless clear, and it is important, because while a service framed with either intention may serve as a stimulus, one which is intended to be followed in detail requires to conform to more stringent psychological laws. It is necessary that those who are responsible for constructing Services should know what they are aiming at, and it is, to say the least, desirable that the members of the congregation should be aware what purpose the spoken prayers are intended to serve.

Communion

Our decision on this issue will depend upon the importance we give to the social aspect of public worship. It seems to me evident that we who lay great stress on the worshipping *fellowship* should be at one with what has hitherto been the main stream of Anglican tradition in holding that our prayers in worship should be *common* prayer. If this is so, then we must seek a method of common worship which will best facilitate the communion of the worshippers with one another, that in unity of mind and spirit with one accord they may worship God. This unanimity is most likely to be attained by the concentration of each and all on the same themes in conjunction with a deliberate identification of the self with the other members of the group, and it will mean, therefore, a definite orientation of the worshipper towards whatever is being done at the moment whether of praise, or petition, or intercession, or the hearing of God's holy word.

As has been remarked earlier, participation in corporate worship requires of the individual self-denial. His own private interests and needs will occupy a secondary place in his mind, and he will (where he can in conscience do so) accommodate himself to the mood and spirit and need of his fellow-worshippers. He will rejoice with those who rejoice, even though his own heart is sorely burdened, and he will sorrow with the sorrowful, even when the lines have fallen unto him in pleasant places.*

But if true corporate worship involves a turning away from the self and a self-identification with the brethren, the renunciation does in fact result in the strengthening and enlargement of the individual who exercises this self-denial. ' It is more blessed to give than to receive.' What is that other than saying that you receive more that way? It is a profound paradox of life. But the giving must be made with single intention. Life will teach us of the recompense which belongs to God's gracious ordering of things. It were an untruth and a culpable self-delusion to pretend that it does not come or that we are indifferent to its coming; yet we cannot seek it without losing it, and giving must be without reserve and with no eye to the reward.

We cannot share with other members of the Christian family without being spiritually enriched by a fuller and deeper apprehension of the Head of the family; we cannot identify ourselves with the prayer and praises of the generations of His children without being strengthened and fortified in the faith, and without realizing the meaning of membership of the

* Cf. Will, op. cit., Vol. I., p. 228 f.

Kingdom in a manner impossible to us in our solitariness.

The argument in favour of detailed participation in a service is supported, further, by the Protestant principle of the priesthood of all believers. It is one thing to be emancipated from the domination of a clerical priesthood; it is quite another to fulfil the ideal of a universal priesthood. We have, Dr. Will claims, driven away the priest without putting the priestly functions into other hands. The proper priest in public worship is the Christian assembly. It cannot exercise its priestly office if it is a passive crowd, constituting a public or an audience rather than a living, active community. Congregational solidarity in the sacerdotal service of prayer is a duty, and that solidarity is, one would think, best achieved by unity of action.*

* Cf. Dr. Will's paper entitled, ' Quelles sont les raisons de la disgrace de nos cultes protestants ? ' in *L'église*, p. 91.

Chapter VII

Prayer the Characteristic of a Whole Service

I

I HAVE said that prayer is the pervading characteristic of the Protestant cultus. Let us turn now to consider this proposition in some detail.

It will be convenient to use as a basis for our discussion the Anglican order for Morning Prayer, especially if we include the sermon and hymns which, strictly speaking, fall outside the Office.

This is not an arbitrary step to take. It is evident that the general structure of an ordinary Free Church Sunday morning or evening service has been strongly influenced by that of the Anglican Mattins and Evensong. The affinities will reveal themselves as we proceed, and the following considerations show it to be extremely improbable that they are due to chance coincidence.

The meetings for worship of the early Separatists seem to have been of a relatively formless character, witness this account of the manner of Barrowist assemblies about 1588 :—

142

' In the sommer tyme they mett together in the fields, a mile or more about London : there they sitt down upon a Banke, and diverse of them expound out of ye Bible so long as they are there assembled. In the winter tyme they assemble themselves by 5 of the clocke in ye morning to that Howse where they make yr conventicle for the Saboth day, men & women together : there they continue in yr kind of prayers and exposition of Scriptures all the day. They dyne together : after dynner make collection to pay for yr dyet & what money is left some one of them carrieth to the prison, where any of their sort be committed. In yr prayer one speaketh, & the rest doe grone, or sob, or sigh, as if they woulde wringe out teares, but say not after him that prayeth : their prayer is extemporall.' *

We may see how Separatist worship gradually developed in form by comparing with the foregoing Cotton Mather's account of the ' usual services which every Lord's Day calleth for ' in New England nearly a hundred and forty years later (1726). I quote Dexter's condensation of pp. 42--62 of Mather's *Ratio Disciplinae*.

* Deposition of Clem. Campbell, *Harleian MS.* 7042, p. 15. Quoted H. M. Dexter, *A Hand-Book of Congregationalism* (Boston, 1880), p. 82.

' 1. The congregations meet twice, at hours " such as they Judge may most suit their edification ".

2. " The Pastor—after the Bills which any of the Neighbours put up, desiring a Remembrance in the Publick Prayers or Praises, on their special Occasions, have been Read—begins with Prayer."

3. " The former and larger Prayer of the Pastor being finished, a Psalm usually succeeds." " Ordinarily the Psalm is read line after line by him whom the Pastor desires to do that service ; and the People generally [that is Congregationally, and not by a choir] sing in such grave Tunes, as are most usual in the churches of our Nation."

4. " The SERMON follows." It is here intimated that the " Sermons of New England " then usually reached " a good way into the second Hour."

5. " The Sermon being finished the Pastor makes a shorter Prayer, wherein he recommends the Sermon, and the principal Documents of it, unto the Operations of the Holy Spirit for the effectual Applications thereof unto the Hearts of the People."

6. " Then—at least in the Afternoon—there is another Psalm sung."

7. " In some of the Congregations, they have

Precisely when the Free Church order came to approximate to the Anglican as closely as it does to-day is a question difficult to answer, and fortunately not a very important one in relation to the purposes of this book. The process of approximation was probably slow and almost certainly not consciously fostered. Principles of order in public worship do not seem to have interested Nonconformists very much. Consequently there was more chance of an established tradition powerfully affecting Nonconformist procedure wherever opportunities occurred for the one to influence the other, for there were no fixed principles which might give rise to opposition. Such occasions of influence were the influx into Nonconformity of the ejected ministers in 1662 and later (and probably more powerful) the Evangelical Revival.

Mattins and Evensong derive directly from the monastic 'Hours' of the Roman Church. Thus Anglican and Nonconformist alike are indebted to the Rule of St. Benedict, drawn up early in the 6th century. Indeed, if he should think in terms of historical pedigree, the Nonconformist at his Sunday Service should sometimes, at least in the secrecy of his heart, make pious acknowledgement of his mother the Church

Clemen, *Quellenbuch zur praktischen Theologie*, Erster Teil, pp. 51 ff.

of England, his grandmother the Church of
Rome, and his great-grandmother the Jewish
Synagogue; and, if his piety will carry him far
enough back, he will remember even the Jerusalem Temple, ancestress of them all.

As is well known, from the time of Constan-
tine, when Christianity became the official and
' correct ' religion, and when consequently men
and women crowded into the Church, vast
numbers of whom were in this act expressing
no radical change of mind and spirit and conscience, there arose within the pale of the
Church what amounted to a double code of
living. There was a ' lower ' way of Christian
life for those—the ' secular '—who threw themselves into the ordinary avocations of the world,
and a ' higher ' way for those—the ' religious '
—who withdrew themselves from the world in
order to live the Christian life in its full purity.
At first, the movement from the ' secular ' to
the ' religious ' life was a reaction of individuals
who fled the temptations of the world to save
their souls in solitariness. The very name
' monk ', i.e. μοναχός, bears witness to this, as
also ' hermit ', or one who dwells in the loneli-
ness of the desert (ἔρημος). In time, however,
a more wholesome practice began to prevail
whereby the ' religious ' would band themselves
together to live under a ' rule ' in a community.

The main duty of these monks ' regular ' (who, it should be borne in mind, were at first chiefly laymen) was to do God's work, the *opus Dei*. ' There was little doubt in Benedict's day ', writes Professor Burkitt, ' as to what this was : it was the perpetual recitation of the divinely inspired hymn-book of the Church, i.e. the Psalms.' *

That this working through of the Psalms is at the heart of the structure of the Anglican Mattins and Evensong is obvious, and Cranmer's indebtedness to the Catholic ' Hours ' becomes clearer still when you observe how the first Office for the day began according to the Benedictine Rule. It started with Ps. li. 15 : † Domine, labia mea aperies : et os meum annunciabit laudem tuam ; or Ps. lxx. 1 : Deus, in adjutorium meum intende : Domine, ad adjuvandum me festina. Then came Ps. iii. followed by a *Gloria* ; and after that Ps. xcv : Venite, exsultemus Domino : jubilemus Deo salutari nostro : &c., followed by six psalms and some readings.‡

The liturgical recitation of the Psalms goes back, of course, through the Synagogue to the Jewish Temple, from which the Synagogue borrowed it. There seems to have been in

* F. C. Burkitt, *Christian Worship*, p. 57. See also pp. 31 ff.   † I follow the versio vulgata.

‡ See F. C. Burkitt, ibid., p. 58.

the Temple Liturgy a special psalm for
each day of the week. On this point Dr.
Oesterley quotes the Mishnah *Tamid* vii. 4, as
follows : ' These were the Psalms which the
Levites used to recite in the Temple; on the
first day of the week they used to recite *The
earth is the Lord's* (xxiv) ; on the second day,
Great is the Lord (xlviii) ; on the third day, *God
standeth in the congregation of the mighty* (lxxxii) ;
on the fourth day, *God of vengeance* (xciv) ; on
the fifth day, *Exult aloud unto God our strength*
(lxxxi) ; on the sixth day, *The Lord reigneth*
(xciii) ; on the Sabbath, *A Psalm, a song for the
Sabbath day* (xcii).' *

In the non-episcopal churches of to-day this
ancient tradition of reciting over a certain period
the whole psalter is no longer followed, but its
impress can still be discerned in the chant which
is a customary item in a Free Church Sunday
Service and in the singing of the paraphrases
which is dear to Scottish Presbyterians.

If the Psalms are not conspicuous in British
Protestant worship outside of the Church of
England, it was not always thus. ' I am grateful ', wrote Dr. Fairbairn, ' that my childhood
was nurtured on the Book of Psalms rather
than on the jingling verses that celebrate the

* W. O. E. Oesterley, *The Jewish Background of the
Christian Liturgy*, p. 74.

" sweet Saviour ", or protest how I love " my Jesus ". Well do I remember the old barn-like meeting-house to which I was taken as a child, and where I went as a boy, with its bare walls, its unpainted windows, its unstained, high-backed, square family pews; the long sermon, the hard, worn, furrowed faces, now, alas ! all turned to dust; the low, stern grumble or high falsetto that then seemed the fittest voice for praise. But one memory to-day drowns and dwarfs all these, the sense that old congregation and those ancestors and kinsfolk of mine had for the majesty of God, and the reality to them of the inspired Psalms to which they owed it.' *

The Psalms themselves were responsible for the number of the Hours † observed by the Religious, as well as forming the basis of the Offices recited. In course of time the Office proper to each Hour was expanded by the addition of prayers and other readings to the recitation of the appointed Psalms.

Cranmer, when he constructed the two daily services of Mattins and Evensong on the model

* A. M. Fairbairn, *Studies in Religion and Theology*, p. 272 f.

† To give the names in present use : Mattins, Lauds, Terce, Sext, Nones, Vespers, Compline. The Scriptural foundation was Ps. cxix. 62, ' At midnight I will rise to give thanks unto thee ', and Ps. cxix. 164, ' Seven times a day do I praise thee.'

of the seven canonical Hours, retained as his framework the recitation of the Psalter, but altered the emphasis by placing it not on this but upon the reading of the Bible as a whole and the exposition of the Word.* His intention will be plain to anyone who reads that refreshing piece of prose which follows the caption ' Concerning the Service of the Church ' in the Book of Common Prayer.

Those interested in liturgical affinities will notice that his ordering of the daily services marks in some respects a closer approximation to the order of worship in the ancient Jewish Synagogue, and to that extent also to the practice of the primitive Church. In this connexion we may compare the Anglican and Free Church services. The Anglican service is nearer to that of the Synagogue in its ' liturgical ' prayers and its recitation of the Psalms; the Free Church is nearer in its avoidance of a fixed Lectionary †

* Vid. F. C. Burkitt on ' The Reformation and Divine Worship ', *The Modern Churchman*, Vol. XXII, Nos. 5, 6, and 7, p. 305.

† This statement needs some modification. At the beginning of the Christian era there was a fixed triennial cycle of weekly readings from the Pentateuch. (See Oesterley, *The Jewish Background of the Christian Liturgy*, p. 39.) There were also readings from the Prophets. Perhaps there were general directions regarding what should be read here, while the amount was left to the judge-

and in the freedom which it allows (at all events in theory) to any suitable person, minister or ' layman ', to select and to expound the readings from Scripture.*

So much by way of preface to our theme. It is well, when we are examining a particular Anglican Service, to have in mind something of the manner in which it is historically conditioned, and also to be aware of the relationship in which a traditional Free Church Service stands to it. Moreover, the bearing of these historical considerations on the suitability of a Service for the end for which it is intended should be plain. We need to ask, for instance, Is a given practice that most appropriate to the purpose in view, or is it retained in fact, though not consciously, because it is a relic of an older order which sought a somewhat different end?

---

ment of the reader. (See Oesterley, ibid., p. 40.) Cf. Lk. iv. 16–21. Was the reading from Isaiah prescribed for the day, but the selection of the particular passage left to Jesus? That would seem to be the inference. It must be admitted that there is surprisingly little that we know beyond doubt of the details of Synagogue worship in the time of Christ. Cf. Dr. P. P. Levertoff's Essay on ' Synagogue Worship in the First Century,' *Liturgy and Worship*, pp. 60 ff.

* The reader and the expositor might be the same person or different persons. Cf. Lk. iv. 16–21 and Acts xiii. 14–16, and vid. Oesterley, op. cit., p. 42.

II

Now let us look at Mattins to see how it substantiates the claim that it is characteristically a service of prayer, using prayer in the full sense of the to and fro commerce between the worshipper and God. For brevity of comment I shall distinguish between the two movements of prayer, from man Godwards and from God manwards, by calling the one man's word and the other God's word. It will be understood that in this particular discussion I shall use these phrases as convenient signs without prejudging the question whether what *represents* God's word is God's word in very truth.

The service begins with Sentences or a Sentence from Scripture.

At once we are in the realm of prayer: God speaks and man speaks. If, for example, the first Sentence is chosen, then the Office begins with God's word: 'When the wicked man turneth away from his wickedness that he hath committed, and doeth that which is lawful and right, he shall save his soul alive.' (Ezek. xviii. 27.) The second Sentence is man's word: 'I acknowledge my transgressions, and my sin is ever before me' (Ps. li. 3); the fourth combines the two: 'The sacrifices of God are a broken spirit : a broken and a contrite heart, O God, thou wilt not despise ' (Ps. li. 17).

It may be thought, perhaps, that my contention here is little more than a quibble. An objector may say that from the point of view of the congregation the reading out of these sentences is not equivalent to leading in an act of real prayer. What the attentive part of the congregation is doing is listening to something which Ezekiel once said with prophetic authority or overhearing the Psalmist in his address to God. The sentences are intended but to set the worshippers' minds moving in a certain direction ; they are simply meant to be stimuli to thought. Up to a point that is true enough ; but then are not all words spoken or sung in a service stimuli with a like purpose ? The worshipper comes to speak to God and to listen to God : he seeks communion. Looked at in one way the uttered words are a formal representation of the many-coloured movements of the spirit in this communion. The importance of this representation lies in its concreteness, in its giving definite form and content to the vague and formless purposes and aspirations of the soul and to the soul's dim apprehensions of the Divine. Some people think that this definiteness acts as a check upon communion with God, because the definite is the limited, and the soul which is to have the richest communion with the Infinite must be free from such trammels. But surely the history of art is a standing refutation of this view. The great artists in all branches of art are the magicians who convey us furthest into the larger realms of the spirit where we feel on our faces the breath of eternity and infinity, and their magic wand is the particular, the concrete embodiment, the power of which is dependent upon the very perfection of its definiteness. In order to enter the new worlds opened up by a work of art we need to ' live ourselves in ' to it. The more we do that the further we travel and the greater number of fresh horizons open up to view. But, this process of ' living ourselves in ' is achieved only by our giving ourselves up to the artistic creation in all its concrete particularity. That is the principle which we should firmly grasp. It applies to our communion with God. There is great virtue in the ' Thus saith the Lord ' of the Hebrew prophets. Doubtless to put statements into the mouth of God may well seem a dangerous and over-bold thing to do, however confident you may be that you are faithfully representing Him, for it is as it were to pin Him down, to limit Him, to narrow Him; and yet it is only by translating His word into the limiting terms which belong to our finitude that it can be conveyed to us with any adequacy at all. Let it be granted that we may come to feel that a particular ' Thus saith the Lord ' of a prophet is but a doubtful expression in words of the Eternal Mind. None the less it remains true that we advance to a deeper understanding of that Mind only by concentrating attention on definite, concrete ' thusnesses '. In so far as the prophet who speaks in the name of the Lord is possessed of a ' pure heart ' (in the sense of that phrase in the Gospels), what he says *is* a means of communication between God and man, effective in the measure that it is received as from God in its clear-cut positiveness, and adequate in the measure that it creates in the hearer a greater sensitiveness to spiritual things.

Now the opening Sentences are a means of getting the communication going, so to speak. They are the water poured into the pump to start it working. They are of the nature of prayer in that they are conducive to the reality of communion. God is heard speaking to man and man is heard speaking to God, and the worshipper who comes to his worship in sincerity not only listens to what is said, but begins to identify himself with the conversation, so that he appropriates to himself what of God's word speaks to his personal need, and, moreover, his mind tends to move Godwards along the lines of the prayer which he is overhearing. He listens, for instance, to the words ' I acknowledge my transgressions, and my sin is ever before me ', and, though he does not, probably, take them as his own in direct address to God, yet he begins to think of himself in the sight of God and his mind begins to move towards a definite prayer of confession; there is a movement of spirit preparatory to the act where, with full consciousness of what he is doing and that it is he who is doing it, he acknowledges to God with his fellow-Christians that he has followed too much the devices and desires of his own heart. The Sentences are thus in the realm of prayer because by formal means they are conducive to the initiation of a living commerce between the worshipper and God, and so bring about a preliminary stage of prayer.

So much for the Scriptural sentences with which Morning Prayer begins. It is, of course, a common practice to start a Free Church service in a similar way, though the passages used are not confined to the selection provided in the Prayer Book.

I intend to discuss later the question of the order of a service and of the manner of conducting the order, but it will not be out of place to raise here a doubt whether the practice in the Church of England and in the Free Churches of standing while the Sentences are recited is the one best adapted to making them effective. I incline to the opinion that few people in fact pay much attention to them, and that at most they serve to create a ' holy ' atmosphere; whereas, if suitable sentences are recited after the congregation has composed itself to the attitude which it usually adopts for prayer, then they become a far more powerful stimulus to active worship and prayer.*

III

After the Sentences follows the familiar call to confession beginning ' Dearly beloved brethren '. It has had many critics. This is not, however, the place to join them even if I were disposed to do so, which I am not. That by endless repetition it has lost all, or almost all, its vitality would, I suppose, be generally conceded. How could it be otherwise? But I should not wish to attend its final obsequies, for it contains the classical statement of the purpose for which we ' assemble and meet together ' in church or chapel : ' to render thanks for the great benefits

* In various communities it has been, I am aware, the practice to pray standing, but it is not at the present day a custom which holds in England.

that we have received at his hands, to set forth his most worthy praise, to hear his most holy Word, and to ask those things which are requisite and necessary, as well for the body as the soul '. Sacrifice—spiritual sacrifice—and communion : those are the ends of a Protestant Service of Prayer.

Next comes the General Confession—man's word—followed by the Absolution (God's word, except that the last part is an exhortation by the priest to the people). Thereafter the Lord's Prayer—man's word—followed by versicles and responses (also man's word) : V. O Lord, open thou our lips. R. And our mouth shall shew forth thy praise. (Ps. li. 15.) V. O God, make speed to save us. R. O Lord, make haste to help us. (Ps. lxx. 1.)

Since the beginning of the Confession the congregation has been kneeling. Now all stand, and minister and people bestir one another to worship. First is said the Gloria Patri, divided responsively, and then the minister says ' Praise ye the Lord ', and the people answer ' The Lord's name be praised '. This leads up to the corporate act of setting forth God's ' most worthy praise ' by reciting or singing the 95th Psalm, Venite, exultemus Domino.*

* For the purposes of the present exposition there is no need to draw attention to exceptional circumstances where a

IV

Before we proceed I would point out how well adapted in form, at all events, this stage of the Office is for the initiation of a service whose essential characteristic is not only prayer but corporate prayer. Whether or not its fixity is admirable is another matter, but as a model establishing in well-balanced proportion those activities and passivities which go to the welding of a group into a worshipping unity there is very much to be said in its favour. The rhythmical alternation between God's word and man's word, the vocal participation of the congregation in the Confession and the Lord's Prayer and the Responses, the dialogue between minister and people—these things make for communion, the communion of the worshippers with one another and of all, individually and corporately, with God. Doubtless no arrangement of words and of ' parts ' will of itself and alone achieve this end. Let the words be gabbled through or the service undertaken listlessly, without reverent attention to meaning and without serious intent to a corporate act, and the service becomes a vain mockery; not a reasonable

---

different order is followed, as, e.g., that here the Venite is not sung at Easter nor on the day when this Psalm is one of the Psalms for the day.

sacrifice, but an outrage upon God, not a unifying act of fellowship, but an act of despite to the Body of Christ. That does not mean, however, that the structure and formal content of a service is of negligible importance. Because many people are foolish enough to get indigestion by bolting their food is no reason for omitting to stir the porridge and add the salt.

There can be little question that the main cause for the absence of dialogue between minister and people in the usual Free Church service is the traditional Nonconformist aversion from the use of a prayer book. A minister can extemporize a prayer or an exhortation, but neither prayers nor responses can be extemporized by a whole assembly acting in unison. A dialogue between an individual and a group is possible only if the speakers know their parts, and a part has to be learnt or read—it cannot be the purely spontaneous expression of the moment. Suspicion of stereotyped formulæ and (for this and other reasons) rejection of a ' book ' are thus the chief historical cause of this lack of dialogue. I fancy, however, that, at least in the latter part of the 19th century and the beginning of the 20th, there was a subsidiary reason making for the perpetuation of the lack, and a reason all the more powerful because it was not, so far as I know, explicitly formulated.

If I am right, it had to do with a growing sentiment which found one mode of expression when (in non-Presbyterian circles) the minister first of all divested himself of gown and bands, and later dispensed with a white tie. There was, I suspect, a vague feeling that to introduce dialogue between minister and people would be to separate the minister from the congregation, to emphasize his ' difference ', even to fortify a conception of the minister as belonging to a priestly caste. It was all right if he did all the speaking while the congregation kept silence, for that was consonant with his being merely the mouthpiece of a group of which he formed part. In a duet, however, one singer is not the mouthpiece of the other.*

The effect of all this is curious : the Puritan Dissenter with his keen assertion of the doctrine of the priesthood of all believers is *in his services of prayer* (that qualification must be marked) far more dependent on the ' medicine-man ' than is his friend of the Episcopal Church who lays

---

* It should be understood that I am referring to the typical Free Church service such as is commonly found in small town or village. In some of the larger churches, especially those which go to the expense of printing a Service paper, versicles and responses are used; but the practice is not sufficiently general to escape remark from a visitor.

great stress on ' orders ' and the Apostolical Succession.

From a psychological point of view the virtue of the congregation's taking an active, vocal part in the prayers, to the end that each member may more fully share in corporate worship, would seem patent. I do not mean that a man cannot pray without breaking into articulate speech ; but definite action, specific outward expression, is a great aid to the concentration of attention on a common purpose, and it is the enemy of vagueness and the wandering mind. And further, what may be called the harmonious rivalry of dialogue between minister and congregation, or, for that matter, between two parts of a congregation, is a powerful agent for welding the assembly into a unified whole and for engendering emotional warmth in relation to the concerns for which it has met together.

' Surely it is time ', wrote C. Silvester Horne and T. H. Darlow in 1897, ' for each congregation to claim its audible share in that public devotion which Free Churchmen should be the last to allow a minister to monopolise '. *

The line taken on this subject by the Puritan Presbyterians in their ' Exceptions against the Book of Common Prayer ' at the Savoy Confer-

* *Let us Pray*, A Handbook of Selected Collects and Forms of Prayer for the Use of the Free Churches, p. 4.

ence of 1661 deserves attention. It doubtless
represents the general Puritan view, Separatist
no less than Presbyterian, and it is instructive
about the reasons which formed the ground of
subsequent Nonconformist practice.

Their third proposal runs as follows :—

' That the repetitions, and responsals of the
clerk and people, and the alternate reading of
the psalms and hymns which cause a confused
murmur in the congregation, whereby what is
read is less intelligible, and therefore unedifying,
may be omitted : the minister being appointed
for the people in all public services appertain-
ing unto God, and the Holy Scriptures, both of
the Old and New Testament, intimating the
people's part in public prayer to be only with
silence and reverence to attend thereunto, and
to declare their consent in the close, by saying
Amen.' *

The disingenuousness of the Bishops' reply
to the Puritans' proposals is notorious, but
there would seem to be some reason in their
retort to this particular one at least. The
Puritans say that responsals and alternate readings should go because they do not edify; the

* *Documents Relating to the Settlement of the Church of
England by the Act of Uniformity of 1662*, Edited by the
Rev. Geo. Gould, p. 114.

Bishops say they should continue ' because they do edify, if not by informing our reasons and understandings . . ., yet by quickening, continuing, and uniting our devotion, which is apt to freeze or sleep, or flat in a long continued prayer or form : it is necessary therefore for the edifying of us therein to be often called upon and awakened by frequent Amens, to be excited and stirred up by mutual exultations, provocations, petitions, holy contentions and strivings, which shall most shew his own, and stir up others' zeal to the glory of God. For this purpose alternate reading, repetitions, and responsals are far better than a long tedious prayer.' * The Bishops then cite ancient practice, Christian and Jewish, and deny that the propriety of the minister's solo part can be proved from Scripture, ending with a spiteful (and largely irrelevant) *argumentum ad hominem*. In one of the Puritans' principal parts of worship, singing of psalms, the people bear as great a part as the minister. ' If this way be done in Hopkins', why not in David's Psalms; if in metre, why not in prose; if in a psalm, why not in a litany ? ' †

The rejoinder of the Puritans to this reply of the Bishops is interesting. There is a pardonable tartness about it. ' What ', they begin,

* ibid., p. 149 f.   † ibid., p. 150.

' is most for edification, is best known by experience, and by the reason of the thing. For the former, you are not the masters of all men's experience, but of your own, and others that have acquainted you with the same, as theirs. We also may warrantably profess in the name of ourselves, and many thousands of sober, pious persons, that we experience that these things are against our edification, and we beseech you do not by us, what you would not do by the poor labouring servants of your family, to measure them all their diet for quality or quantity, according to your own appetites, which they think are diseased, and would be better if you worked as hard as they.' *

After stating their experience, they appeal to Scripture as a ground of their judgement. The modern English Nonconformist will find their argument strange reading. Here is part of it. ' I. Though we have not said that the people may not in psalms to God concur in voice (we speak of prayer which you should have observed) and though we only concluded it agreeable to the Scripture practice, for the people in prayer to say but their Amen; yet knowing not from whom to understand the will of God, and what is pleasing to him, better than

* ibid., p. 236.

from himself, we considered what the Scripture saith of the ordinary way of public worship; and finding ordinarily that the people spoke no more in prayer (as distinct from psalms and praise) than their Amen, or mere consent, we desired to imitate the surest pattern. 2. As we find that the minister is the mouth of the people to God in public (which Scripture, and the necessity of order do require), so we were loth to countenance the people's invading of that sacred office, so far as they seem to us to do;— 1. By reading half the psalms and hymns;— 2. By saying half the prayers, as the minister doth the other half;—3. By being one of them the mouth of all the rest in the confession at the Lord's Supper;—4. By being the only petitioners, in the far greatest part of all the litany, by their good Lord deliver us, and we beseech thee to hear us good Lord. While the minister only reciteth the matter of the prayer, and maketh none of the request at all, we fear lest, by parity of reason, the people will claim the work of preaching, and other parts of the ministerial office.' * They next restate their objection on the ground that the confused murmur of voices is unedifying, and then pull to pieces the Bishops' citations from ancient practice, finally dealing trenchantly with the

* ibid., p. 237.

Bishops' intentionally offensive distinction between Hopkins' and David's psalms.

When the Puritans appeal to experience and say that they and those whom they represent find the responsals unedifying, the rational view to take is that they are better without the said responsals, and a modern man would hold it monstrous to force them on them. A worshipping group itself is the only competent authority to decide what is and what is not edifying to it. We should remember, however, that while it may have been perfectly true that the responsals as conducted in the parish churches at that time were unedifying, it does not follow that responsals in whatever way conducted are always unedifying.

While they stand on the firm ground of their own experience there can be no gainsaying of the Puritans. The Presbyterians say, Our experience is this; the Bishops say, Our experience is the direct opposite. It is useless to dispute with either party. But when reasons are given for the experience we move at once into a realm where argument has its proper place, and in that realm on this particular issue the Puritans are more often amusing than convincing. They have, indeed, one cogent argument, but it is cogent in its bearing on conditions in the 17th century and not on conditions in the 20th. The confused murmur of voices is unintelligible to those members of the congregation who, because they have not learnt their part or because they cannot read, are unable themselves to join in. To them it is unedifying. These brethren must be considered, and all things must be done unto edification. That is a very reasonable argument; but the conclusions from Scripture are to-day seen to be palpably illegitimate, while the reasons drawn from the danger of the people's invasion of the minister's sacred office would make even our present-day sacerdotalists smile.

This controversy is not simply a matter of antiquarian interest. It has affected Free Church practice ever since, and, if we are to conserve what is valuable and change what is obsolete in our tradition, we need to be aware of it and to be aware of the reasons which made the Puritans so strong in their contention.

For generations the only audible part taken by a Free Church congregation in a service of worship has been the singing of psalms and hymns and the repetition of the Lord's Prayer. (The meticulous will point to exceptions, but this is an almost universally valid generalization.) Even the Amen which, conformably to Scripture, the Puritans assigned to the people has for long been spoken by the minister alone, thus serving as little more than an indication to the listless that it is time for them to ' come to ' again.

The point that needs to be made is that this tradition of congregational mutism took its rise from considerations which however forcible at the time are without force to-day. For a generation in which all can read the charge that a confused murmuring is unedifying because it is unintelligible to the hearers falls to the ground (for it will hardly be urged that God finds it confusing !) ; for a generation which has advanced in historical sense the argument from Scripture is quite unconvincing ; and for a generation nurtured in democracy the notion that the worshipper should be kept in his place is not one which will be embraced with enthusiasm.

Free Churchmen should shake themselves free from the trammels of traditions based on reasons no longer operative. The tradition, of course, may have been good, though the reasons were poor, and in that event let the tradition prevail. Experience must decide, but it should be experience arising out of honest search and experiment, and not the experience which is the result of inertia and a blind clinging to tradition because what is customary requires the least effort.

Dialogue in a service, as we have seen, cannot be spontaneous; but it does not follow from this that it cannot be varied, and if it is to be living one would have thought that it must be varied. Mr. C. E. Watson states the Free Church point of view here admirably when he says that the supreme danger of liturgical use is 'the staling of words by their constant repetition'. 'No particular form', he continues, 'however excellent or appropriate may safely be employed with great frequency. The Anglican Book of Common Prayer which, as a classic, is rightly regarded with veneration, can only profitably be followed by us generally and at a respectful distance. It looks back, and not only in word and phrase, it looks back to a generation that could not read and consequently had to know the service by heart. One order for the morning, and one for the evening, might, in these circumstances, be inevitable. How they can be endured to-day it is hard to understand.' *

A number of prayer books, containing a variety of services in part 'responsive', for the use of Free Churches have been issued. They differ in excellence or, some would say, in degree of inferiority. It is common for ministers to speak of them with mild disparagement, and then to use them—but not for the purpose for

* See the preface to the *Rodborough Bede Book*.

which they were compiled, namely to be used by the congregation as well as by the minister as an aid to really common worship in which all take their part audibly.

Hitherto none of these books has 'taken on' at all widely—not even (in Congregational Churches) the *Book of Congregational Worship*, published by the Congregational Union of England and Wales, and therefore free from any suspicion of 'Catholicizing' tendency. I believe that one reason why they have not had more success than they have is that, whatever their individual merits, they one and all in their different ways fail to express the special quality of Free Church worship through the forms which they provide. That quality I will not be rash enough to try to define, though I am confident it exists. I should say that it manifests itself negatively in a dislike of archaisms whose details must be ignored and whose general meaning must be forced if they are to be made to express with the right accent the genuine sentiment of the worshippers, and that it manifests itself positively in a demand for the clear expression of those feelings and desires which belong to the particular time and circumstance and which may find a legitimate place in worship.

We do not object to the archaic because it is old. There are classic expressions of Christian piety which belong to all time, and whose value is immeasurably enhanced because they do not belong simply to the present age, but link the worshipper in thought and feeling with the Church of all time. These are not alien to the spirit of the Free Churches—which is not, of course, to say that the Free Churches in fact make the use they might of the treasures available. Furthermore, the demand that modern needs should be expressed in current terms is not a demand either for colloquial language or for a matter-of-fact prosiness. There is an exaltation of language natural to worship; it is akin to poetry, though it would be misleading to call it ' literary '. Though you may miss it in many a Nonconformist chapel, yet, when you find it, you will be listening to the genuine accents of Free Church worship.

But to return to the prayer books. Undoubtedly many Nonconformists would say that the reason why they fail to express the special quality of Free Church worship is just that they are prayer books and that they do provide forms.

Is that the truth? Is it really true that Free Churches cannot employ the most congregational of all means of public worship without being subtly false to the principles of worship for which they stand? A strange paradox indeed ! The question, let it be understood, is not whether there shall be extemporary prayer, but whether a place shall be found in the service for the vocal participation of the congregation in the prayers. Can the characteristic quality of Free Church worship not find expression through any written forms ?

Before that question is answered in the negative it would be well if a large number of churches gave a year's serious trial to the *Rodborough Bede Book*, already referred to. It is not at all like an ordinary Service Book, but it provides a great number and variety of short responsive offices which can be selected as a hymn is selected to suit a particular place in the Service. It is not a ' precious ' book, but is the fruit of labour in a very living and very congregational Congregational Church. It is wealthy in what is Scriptural, what is classically Christian, and what is modern. The liturgical purist will not like it, but that is not because it is compiled by one who is ignorant of the canons of liturgical rectitude; the compiler has sought to meet the needs of folk who are not, and never will be, liturgiologists, and he has deliberately put the demands of to-day before those of a traditional correctness. Use alone will test its value, but it must be the use for which it has been made, and not that of serving as yet another source-book for ministers.*

V

We now come back to Mattins and the *Venite* which had just been reached.

It would be possible to make a fairly successful analysis of the psalms and hymns on the basis of the distinction we have used between God's word and man's word, but the enterprise would be a little forced and hardly of much profit. In order to show that they belong to the realm of prayer it is sufficient to point out that (provided they are worthy) they lift our hearts up to God.† That they do by setting forth His praise, by declaring His mighty acts, and by addressing Him directly in the second person singular, deliberately using an artistic medium. Beauty is spiritual. Where Beauty is apprehended by means of a concrete embodiment of the beautiful there at least the outer

* Only the poorest churches should be unable to raise the money necessary for the experiment, for, thanks to a Christian patron who cares not to let his left hand know what his right hand doeth, copies of the Bede Book can be had at a remarkably low price if not less than fifty are ordered.   Enquiries should be made to the Revd. C. Ernest Watson, Rodborough, Stroud, Glos.

† Cf. the words of Bucer quoted by Will, op. cit., Vol. I., p. 286.

courts of prayer have been reached; for is not beauty the robe of God? The hymns, then, in so far as they are of æsthetic value, belong in virtue of their art to prayer.* Further, when they are the expression of the living religious consciousness of the congregation, they become a *spiritual sacrifice*—the highest form of sacrifice, which is prayer. They are also prayer when they serve to arouse a sense of God's presence, and by awakening religious feeling and moral insight to stir the consciences of the worshippers.† They may, therefore, be prayer as giving form and content to a sacrifice of praise, and they may be prayer in the form of dialogue between man and God.

That the 95th is a felicitous Psalm for the opening act of praise will scarcely be denied. By its structure and content it is especially well fitted to excite the spirit of common worship.

Exception is often taken to the last four verses. Certainly the Psalm can be made to end suitably enough at verse 7. Verses 1–7 form an artistically complete poem in themselves, and only a neurotic fear of omission will insist violently on the continuation of the Psalm to the end. On the other hand, there is something to be said on religious grounds for the retention of the final verses. They constitute

† Cf. Will, ibid., pp. 289 ff.   * Cf. Will, ibid., p. 298 f.

a warning which those who enjoy services fail to heed at peril of soul, and they come at a point where they are most likely to be effective in their abrupt contrast of key, namely where the worshipper is just beginning to be ' warmed up ' to the service.

The danger of worship is the danger which besets all æsthetic experience; it is that of the enjoyment of the Good, the Beautiful, and the True becoming a substitute for the doing of the Good, the Beautiful, and the True. Earlier on it was urged that worship properly understood is an end in itself and that it is greatly impoverished if it is regarded chiefly as a means to something else. I hold to that as a fundamental principle. But there is another principle no less important, and that is the principle of the integrity of life. We fulfil ourselves in action; thought and emotion are a menace to the personality unless they bear issue in action. This does not mean that they should always be deliberately directed towards action as their end, but that, since a wholesome life is all of a piece, intellectual and æsthetic experiences must be related to the activities of the will in daily living, or otherwise there will be a partitioning off of different psychical processes which is inimical to an integrated personality. There is therefore spiritual value in the sudden and sharp reminder, after we have stirred one another to worship Him who is the Maker of all things visible, and not only our Maker, but also our Shepherd : ' To-day if ye will hear his voice, harden not your hearts '. A quickened sense of the nature of God and of His presence is indeed beautiful and good, and it is very meet, right, and our bounden duty to give it expression in praise, but if the vision and the emotional warmth are not carried over into obedience the soul is indulging in a sentimentality whose end is spiritual death.

The conception of Yahweh ' swearing in his wrath ', taken at its face value, is certainly not Christian; but if we are to use the old Hebrew Psalms at all, we must reconcile ourselves to the use of pre-Christian images by bearing in mind their origin in the history of religious thought and by interpreting them in a manner consonant with Christian ideas. There are, it may be agreed, many places where they are so flagrantly contrary to Christian thought that the interpretation cannot be made without forcing them to such an extent that a straight-forward mind feels that there is no genuine relationship between the interpretation and the original image. Where this is so the image is a hindrance, not an aid, to Christian worship, and a sensitive conscience will rightly reject it. But I do not think the passage we are considering is of this nature. If there are sure spiritual truths, this one is sure, that without obedience to the Divine voice we cannot in the God-given nature of things enter into the Divine rest. Nevertheless, if by reason of a lack of historical sense or through a prosaic matter-of-factness of mind people are offended by these last four verses and suppose that the singing or recitation of them by Christians implies an affirmation of them at their face value, then no doubt it will be wiser to strike them out.

At the close of the Venite, as of all the other Psalms, the Gloria Patri is sung or said as the case may be. 'The purpose', writes Mr. E. C. Ratcliff, ' of the doxology is to turn the Psalms and canticles of the Old Testament into Christian hymns, by affirming belief in the God who, though only fully revealed in Trinity to the Church of the New Testament, is nevertheless truly known by the Church of the Old.' The practice apparently goes back at least as far as the end of the fourth century.*

* Vid. *Liturgy and Worship*, p. 271 f.

VI

In a Free Church morning Service the place of the Venite is commonly taken by a hymn of praise. Frequently this hymn owes its inspiration to the Psalms, and sometimes it is simply a metrical version of one of them. I refer, of course, to modern practice.

The history of hymn-singing in this country since the Reformation is long, complicated, and often very diverting. One or two features of it must be noted here to be sure that we have our bearings, but this is not the place to survey the whole field, which can be done by reference to the recognized authorities.*

It has been said that Lutheran Germany sang itself into the Reformation. The same could not be said with equal force of England or Scotland, although doubtless even here singing played some part in the process, and later on it played a very large part in the growth and consolidation of Protestantism. Thanks to the genius of Luther the growth and development of hymnody can be observed from the beginning in Germany, whereas in England, Scotland, and France the influence of Geneva prevailed, and

* Vid., *e.g.*, Frere's ' Introduction ' in the Historical Edition of *Hymns Ancient and Modern*, and Part I of J. Spencer Curwen's *Studies in Worship-Music*.

instead of the *chorale* we find the metrical psalm.

The creator of the modern English hymn was the Independent, Isaac Watts,* who was not born until 1674. In 1700 Enoch Watts, his brother, wrote and urged him to ' revive the dying devotion of the age ' by publishing the hymns which he had written four or five years previously.† His hymns were published in 1707, and they were followed by his psalms in 1719. On this latter book let me quote J. Spencer Curwen :

' The glow of spiritual delight that passed through the Independent Churches as this book came to be diffused among them was not due to the fact that Dr. Watts had made a new translation of the Psalms of David. Tate and Brady, Dr. Patrick, and others had done this, without reviving the spirit of the psalmody. The work that Dr. Watts did was to Christianise the Psalms. To use his own words, he imitated them in the language of the New Testament, and applied them to the Christian state and

* Vid. Frere, op. cit., p. lxxxiii : ' He was the creator of the modern English hymn ; which is neither an Office Hymn like Wither's or Ken's or Austin's, nor yet a metrical psalm, nor again a close paraphrase of Scripture, but a new species, evolved from the last named, and acquiring in the process a novel liberty of treatment and a balanced artistic form.'

† J. Spencer Curwen, op. cit., p. 44.

worship. " 'Tis not ", he writes to Cotton
Mather, March 17th, 1717–8, " a translation of
David that I pretend, but an imitation of him
so nearly in Christian hymns that the Jewish
Psalmist may plainly appear, and yet leave
Judaism behind." No one before had done
this. For a century and a half metrical psalmody had been used. " During that time," say
Bennett and Bogue, " the Protestant people of
England, while in their prayers and in their
sermons they were Christians, in their praises
were little better than Jews. Many an eminent
believer, who joined in the public worship for
fifty years, never sang the name of Jesus till
he arrived in heaven." ' *

How different this from Germany, where as
early as the first quarter of the 16th century
the people were singing ' Es ist das heyl uns
kommen her ', ' Chrystum wir sollen loben
schon ', ' Gelobt seystu Jesu Christ ', ' Jesus
Christus unser Heiland, der von uns den Zorn
Gottes wand ', &c.,† and where from that time
on there was a steady stream of hymn-writers,
culminating in the 17th century with the man
whom Dr. Schweitzer calls ' the king of hymn-
writers ', Paul Gerhardt (1607–1676).‡

* J. Spencer Curwen, op. cit., p. 44 f.
† Vid. Schweitzer, *J. S. Bach*, Engl. Trans. by Ernest
Newman, Vol. I., p. 8. ‡ ibid., p. 12.

In the reign of Elizabeth, when the Reformation had become established in this country, the English Church adopted from Geneva the practice of singing metrical psalms—a practice which became so prevalent that ' Psalm singer ' did duty as another name for Protestant.*
' Psalms ', according to Bp. Burnet, ' were much sung by all who loved the Reformation; and it was a sign by which men's affections to that work were measured whether they used to sing them or not.' † The metrical version of the Psalms which held sway in the Church of England from Elizabeth's reign to the close of the 17th century was that of Sternhold and Hopkins, otherwise the ' Old Version ', as it later came to be called to distinguish it from the ' New Version ' of Tate and Brady completed in 1696. During most of its history it was printed as a semi-official appendix to the Prayer Book. ‡

It should be noted in passing that these metrical psalms bound up with the Prayer Book were the forerunners of the modern hymn (out of which the latter grew) in that they were extra-liturgical. The Roman Offices had contained hymns, but they were as fixed for the

* Vid. Curwen, op. cit., p. 1.
† Quoted Curwen, ibid.
‡ Vid. Frere, op. cit., p. xxxix.

particular Office as were the Psalms, Lessons, and Prayers. These metrical psalms, on the contrary, were selected for the occasion as hymns are chosen to-day. The Clerk would decide what verses were to be sung out of a long Psalm—a custom which enabled one official of this class whose wrath had been kindled to announce : ' We shall now sing to the praise and glory of God the one hundred and nineteenth Psalm—the whole on it ! ' The singing of these Psalms was not a substitute for the reading of the prose version of the Psalms for the day, which was a fixed part of the liturgy.

The violent reaction of the extremer Puritans against prescribed forms led some of the early Separatists to reject the singing of even the metrical Psalms, and we find some adopting the most unrelenting Quaker doctrine concerning the conduct of corporate worship. Worship must be wholly spiritual; it must be directed by the Holy Spirit throughout; and that was taken to imply that it must be strictly *ex tempore* throughout. There might be singing ' by gift of the Spirit ', but that could be accomplished only by a brother getting up and extemporizing both words and tune. The practice, however, never became prevalent, owing, doubtless, to what J. S. Curwen calls ' the extreme difficulty, if not the impossibility, of this exercise ',* and consequently amongst those who held this extreme view of spiritual worship singing was ruled out, save that a brother might perhaps be allowed, if moved by the Spirit, to sing a Psalm out of his head without the aid of a book.†

This uncompromising doctrine was not characteristic of Independency as a whole. On the contrary, psalm-singing seems to have been widespread, and it was fostered by such leaders as Ainsworth and Robinson, the former of whom was himself the author of a version of the Psalms published at Amsterdam in 1612. In the preface to this version Ainsworth 'remarks that he finds no tunes for the Psalms set of God, so that each people is to use the most grave, devout, comfortable manner of singing they know.' ‡

There is ground for supposing that in the days of persecution singing may sometimes have been avoided for the sake of safety. J. S. Curwen quotes a significant sentence from a Church record dated 1682 : 'April 1st, we met at Mr. Russell's in Ironmonger Lane, where Mr. Lambert, of Deadman's Place, Southwark, admin-

---

* Op. cit., p. 41.

† ' We hold ', said John Smyth, ' that seeing singing a psalm is a part of spiritual worship, it is unlawful to have the book before the eye in time of singing a psalm '. (Quoted Curwen, ibid.)   ‡ ibid.

istered to us the ordinance of the Lord's supper, and we sang a psalm in a low voice.' *

As might be inferred from the attitude of John Smyth, the early Baptists were generally averse from congregational singing, although there were exceptions, notable amongst them being the famous Church at Broadmead, Bristol, which employed it to great purpose in diddling the civil authorities.†

A Baptist protagonist of psalm-singing was Benjamin Keach, pastor of the Church at Horsleydown, who entered on his ministry in 1668. We can see the sort of arguments adduced against the practice in the records of his controversy with Isaac Marlowe, a member of the Church; *e.g.*, Christ never sang David's Psalms, which were for the Temple service; formal singing is the same as formal prayer; women ought not to sing in church because they are not allowed to speak there, and because singing is a kind of teaching ; and so on.

We need not stop to see how Keach dealt with these and similar objections, but it is interesting to note that he appealed to the long practice of ' our brethren of the Independent and Presbyterian persuasion ' in support of his contentions, thus providing evidence of the prevalence of psalm-singing in these two bodies.‡

* ibid., p. 43.　　† Vid. ibid., pp. 48 f.　　‡ ibid., pp. 50f.

I have turned aside from our main theme to touch upon these historical matters because it is well to remember how practices have changed with changing times and changing demands. The stereotyped recurrence of hymns which is such a familiar feature of the modern Nonconformist Service is not one which has marked the Nonconformist Service from the beginning.

VII

The Venite is followed by the appointed Psalms for the day, which nowadays are commonly chanted, though where singing cannot be compassed they are read responsively, as was, I take it, the usual post-Reformation practice in parish churches until about a century ago.

There is here, of course, a notable difference between Anglican and Free Church ways. The Free Churches have broken completely away from the Catholic tradition of the regular recitation of the Psalter. If, therefore, we are to keep our parallel going (and I believe the parallel is a real one) we must say that a hymn of praise normally takes the place of the Venite plus the Psalms for the day.

After the Psalms a lesson from the Old Testament or the Apocrypha is read. The lesson is prescribed by the official lectionary.*

It is customary at the corresponding place in a Nonconformist Service for a lesson to be read. Until recently it would be a lesson from the Old Testament, to be followed after singing, as in the Anglican Service, by a lesson from the New Testament. To-day in a large number of chapels there is only one lesson, and that may be taken either from the Old or from the New Testament. About this change I shall have something to say presently. For the moment I would draw attention to the importance of following an ordered series of readings throughout the year.

The Bible is not read and meditated upon as it once was by English Protestants. Unfortunately the minister will be wise to assume ignorance on the part of many in his congregation even of the details of the Gospels. More important than ever is it, therefore, that the people should have an opportunity of gaining a coherent acquaintance with the Bible in church. 'The Lord's people', says the *Book of Common Order* of the United Church of Canada, 'should hear the great passages of Scripture at least once a year.' It surely is the duty of a

* Nowadays there is an alternative table of revised lessons officially sanctioned.

minister to make that possible; but that will not be while Scripture readings are chosen haphazard to suit more or less the subject he has taken it into his head to preach about. Granted that it is well that sermon and lessons should have a bearing upon one another, but in these times of our ignorance it were better as a general rule that the subject of the sermon arose out of an ordered series of lessons than that the lessons should be selected now here now there in order to fit in with the theme which the preacher has hit upon for his discourse. I say ' as a general rule ', for the Free Church minister will rightly refuse to be bound down to a rigid following of any table of lessons, even if he should have drawn up the table himself. A special occasion may demand a special subject for the sermon and special readings to go with it, and when that is so, away with the calendars.

The Revised Lectionary of the Church of England has considerable merits, chief of which perhaps are that, in the words of the Revd. J. A. Quail, it ' does at least recognize some of the assured results of modern Biblical science, and it does cover the ground '.* But if the Lord's people are to hear the great passages of Scripture at least once a year, it cannot be adopted as it stands by the Free Churches, for

* *Congregational Quarterly*, Vol. VIII., No. 3, p. 338.

the simple reason that it is constructed on the basis of two services daily throughout the year, and, as Mr. Quail says, whatever may be the practice of Anglicans 'Free Church habit, . . . far from requiring fourteen services a week, tends more and more towards satisfaction with only one, and that one not with unfailing regularity '.* 'The lectionary ', he continues, ' really required to meet the conditions which obtain in the Free Churches to-day is one which shall be so framed that even the " oncer " shall by means of it receive some impression of the continuity and majestic scope, the rich variety and the growing force, of Divine revelation as embodied in the Bible.' †

In the article in the *Congregational Quarterly* from which I quote Mr. Quail himself offers a specimen lectionary for forty Sundays (two lessons for the morning and two for the evening each Sunday). It deserves careful study, for it has been drawn up with much thought and care. Two somewhat opposed impressions affect me on glancing through it. The first is : how much connected reading can be accomplished this way with lessons of no excessive length ; and the second, and perhaps stronger, is : what a mere taste of the whole riches of the Bible can be

* *Congregational Quarterly*, Vol. VIII., No. 3, p. 338.
† ibid., p. 339 f.

given in the compass of a year in this manner.
One criticism waits to be made. The Old Testament lessons for the morning are all drawn from
the Psalms. Is that not wasting an opportunity ?
For the Psalms as a rule can be sung, and if a
Psalm is substituted for a hymn, room is made
for a lesson taken from other portions of the
Old Testament.

The *Book of Common Order* of the Canadian
Church, following its principle that ' the great
passages of Scripture ' should be heard annually,
provides a *Table of Lessons* ' confined largely
to those central passages that gather closely
about : (1) Christ's work of Redemption (Advent
to Pentecost, half the year), and (2) the application of that work to believers (Pentecost to
Advent, the other half of the year)'. * This
lectionary does not provide a fixed series of
Old Testament and New Testament lessons for
two services each Sunday of the year, but for
each Sunday there is a group of two or three
or sometimes more lessons, one at least of which
is taken from the Gospels. Following it, a
minister can thus insure the reading of ' the
great passages ' (or, since there was never an
anthology regarded by everybody as perfect,
perhaps we had better say a goodly and intelligent selection of them), and at the same time

* p. v.

usually be free to find for himself one lesson suitable to the intention of the service as a whole or, perhaps, more particularly to the theme of his sermon. With each group is set down a prayer for grace akin in thought to the passages belonging to the group.

Those who desire help in the construction of a co-ordinated series of lessons throughout the year will do well to consult also the lectionary given in the Presbyterian *Book of Common Order 1928*. In addition to a table providing an ample selection of lessons for the special occasions of the year there are two separate series for ordinary Sundays, the New Testament lesson being regarded as the leading subject, the purpose of the Old Testament lesson being to serve as a background to it.

Mention should be made also of one further book which, if it is studied with attention, will be studied with profit, and that is the book of prayers and Bible readings by the Swedish professor, Dr. Emanuel Linderholm. It can be had in German translation by Th. Reissinger under the title *Neues Evangelienbuch* with a valuable introduction by Dr. Rudolf Otto. The book is constructed on a three-year basis as regards the readings from the Gospels and the Epistles, and for each Sunday there is a passage (often very brief) both from the Psalms and also from other parts of the Old Testament, as a rule the Prophets. The lessons are arranged according to the following scheme : first half-year (Advent to Pentecost), Historia Salutis oder Offenbarung des Reiches Gottes; second half-year, Ordo Salutis oder Ordnung und Vollendung des Reiches Gottes. A minister harassed to decide the themes for his Sunday Services might do far worse than submit himself to the discipline of Linderholm.

Often in the English Church the Lessons are read by a ' layman '. It is a pity this custom is found only rarely in the Free Churches. Doubtless there is a reason for this. In old days the minister not only read the Scripture but also provided a running commentary on what he was reading. Naturally he kept this part of the service in his own hands. In favour of his continuing to do so it may be urged that to-day many Lessons would be more profitable if they were preceded by a word of introduction. That is true ; and when they are of this nature it is perhaps well that the minister should take them and supply whatever introduction is desirable. Let us hope, however, that the running commentary will not come in again. The Bible speaks most clearly when it is allowed to speak for itself. To intersperse a fine passage with note and gloss is to commit an act of desecration, and no intelligent congregation should permit it. That being so, there is no reason why the minister should always read the Lessons, and there are some tolerably good reasons why he should not. Three may be mentioned here. I put them in what is perhaps an ascending order of importance. It is to be assumed, of course, that the reader can read clearly and intelligently. First, many find a change of voice in the speaking part of a service a relief from monotony and a stimulus to attention. Secondly, the corporate feel of a service is strengthened by the outward participation of members of the congregation in its conduct. And thirdly, when ' laymen ' are accustomed to stand up and read the Lessons in church they are more likely to go a step further and to be prepared on occasion to be responsible for other parts of the service; and thus the practice may be urged in the interests of the needed revival of ' lay-praying ' and ' lay-preaching '.

VIII

We return to Mattins. After the First Lesson there is sung or said either the Te Deum Laudamus or the canticle Benedicite, Omnia Opera.

Traditionally the hymn *Te Deum* has been ascribed to St. Augustine and St. Ambrose, but there seems to be no good ground for this ascription, and modern scholarship favours its attribution to Niceta, Bp. of Remesiana (4th cent.).* Originally it ended at verse 21, i.e., with the words 'Make them to be numbered with thy saints in glory everlasting'. The remaining verses do not all belong to the same date. Observe that as the *Te Deum* is a Christian Trinitarian hymn the Gloria is not sung after it.

The *Benedicite* is the 'Song of the Three Children', taken from the Greek addition to Daniel iii. As, like the Psalms, it is Jewish, not Christian, in origin, it is concluded in the Prayer Book by the Gloria.† Mr. Ratcliff remarks that 'the length and monotonous form of *Benedicite* do not commend it for frequent use to modern congregations', and I do not think we shall gainsay him.

At the place in a Free Church service corresponding to that of the *Te Deum* at Mattins it is common to chant a Psalm or a canticle or the *Te Deum* itself.

Next in the Anglican Office comes the Second Lesson, which is taken from the New Testa-

* Vid. E. C. Ratcliff in *Liturgy and Worship*, p. 273.

† This conclusion was first inserted in the Prayer Book of 1549. In the Breviaries the canticle ended with a special doxology of its own. Vid. Ratcliff, ibid., p. 274.

ment. This was once a good Nonconformist tradition also, but towards the close of the 19th century there began to grow up in Nonconformist churches the practice of substituting an address to the children for the Second Lesson, and to-day that practice, though not invariable, is firmly established.

IX

A lively concern for the children is surely Christian and admirable, but it is to be doubted whether this is a laudable way of giving it expression. In the first place, it is unfortunate that the Bible should be silenced in the interests of more ministerial talk, however excellent that talk may be (and it may be excellent if given by a man with a knack for speaking to children). Cutting out Scripture reading for the sake of one more address by the minister is a symptom of that disease to which the Nonconformist minister seems peculiarly susceptible, namely the obsession that his dominant duty in church is to instruct and edify. When the disease obtains a secure hold it becomes an unmitigated pestilence, as all should know who ever came to a service to meet with God and, instead, had to endure being talked at not only in the sermon and the children's address but even in the prayers.

It seems to me significant that the children's address has found a place by ousting one Lesson, but that is not the only means of entrance, and therefore it does not suffice to constitute a fatal objection. No, a more serious objection is that in at least ninety-nine cases out of a hundred this item is fatal to the unity of a service. I use the word ' item ' advisedly, for I think the address to the children is not seen to be intolerable just because a service is conceived as a series of ' items ' and not as an organic whole. One of the radical defects of many a Free Church Service is that it has been drawn up as the programme for a popular concert is drawn up. As with the concert, there is a general conventional order, and within the broad framework of that order an effort is made to fit individual items which shall be attractive in and for themselves, and so to arrange them that the contrasts between them shall keep up the interest. Often it would seem that the minister tackles his Service somewhat as follows : Here are some good opening sentences : we will start with them. Next must come a prayer of ' invocation ', and perhaps I had better add confession of sins. Now it is time for a hymn . . . let me see, this will do excellently, the words are bright, and the choir loves the tune. Then we must have a lesson . . . here's a fine passage . . . no, it's all right, we did not have it last Sunday. It's the people's turn again now . . . they're fond of a well-known chant; what about the Te Deum this morning? Now a story for the children; * and so on. In a service constructed in this manner it is possible for each item to be unexceptionable in and by itself, yet the total effect of the items combined is, to borrow a phrase from Mr. T. L. Harris, little other than that of ' a kind of sacred vaudeville '.†

But the proper purpose of a service is not to provide members of a congregation with a spiritual, or semi-spiritual, meal of varied fare to suit all tastes, but to enable worshippers to take part in a great corporate Act—an Act, it is true, which has many and varied elements in its construction, yet so arranged and co-ordinated that they are built up into one living whole. This means that a service must be a logical, or, if not a logical, at all events a dramatic, unity.‡

* In many churches the position of the ' minister's prayer ' is transposed so that it follows the chant and immediately precedes the ' story to the children '— an arrangement more liturgically inept it is difficult to conceive.

† Vid. T. L. Harris, *Christian Public Worship*, p. 63 f.

‡ Cf. Mr. Harris's remark : ' The Canon of the Roman Mass defies logical analysis but is, I think, dramatically sound '. Op. cit., p. 65.

My own experience of children's addresses (which I have no reason to suspect of being an abnormal one) is that they almost invariably constitute an isolated piece, unrelated to what precedes or what follows in the service, save only to the children's hymn, and not always to that. They do not belong to the rhythm and movement of an Office of worship. The emotional vagaries and ethical problems of animated tables and chairs, kettles, saucepans, and pokers, or the moral lesson to be derived from ' there was once a little boy who . . .' —these things, admirable enough in their place, facilitate neither the setting forth of God's most worthy praise nor the hearing of His most holy word. At best the children are both interested and ' improved '.

About that two things may be said : first, there are other and more suitable occasions for improving them ; and second, if they cannot be kept from boredom except by the introduction of a purely extrinsic interest, then either they should not be made to be present at the service or the service should be so constructed as to be intrinsically interesting to them.

What valid reasons are there for bringing a child to church unless they be that he himself may learn the rudiments of worship and that he himself may be set upon the way to communion with God? To these high ends there is no means equal to the impress of a worshipping people. A child is sensitive to environment. If, when he attends a service, he finds his elders moved by a spirit of awe and reverence, wonder and adoration, he will make a discovery which no number of talks from the minister could reveal to him, and a discovery of more value to him than many social and ethical precepts.

If children are to attend ordinary ' grown-up ' services (and there is much to be said for their doing so, especially if they come with their parents), then it is certainly good that they should have a part of the service into which they can enter as their very own. But that they may learn to worship, and also that they may be fully interested, that part should be active rather than passive, doing rather than listening. The children's hymn, it is true, belongs to such activity, but by itself it is hardly sufficient for their spiritual demands. There should be prayers—and not only the Lord's Prayer—in which they can join audibly, whether with responses or by praying vocally with minister and congregation; and it should not be beyond the power of a living church to provide scope for other simple activities in which they can join.

We do well to remember that, whatever the adult Puritan may be, the child is naturally a little ceremonialist. He expresses himself through his body, through bodily activity, and he learns through his own activity and through watching the activities of others. Moreover, he enjoys the formal and dignified, and he puts a wealth of meaning into it not easily realized by the sophisticated adult.

If we wish to teach him the central significance in life of the worship of God, and to enable him to awake to the sublimity of the divine Presence, we should be willing to fit our actions to the expression of our hearts, because the child depends so largely upon action for the attainment of insight. My plea is not for a gorgeous ceremonial, but for simple and grave expression in outward act of what I must assume is the inward movement of the spirit. We may be able to pray as truly and as reverently doubled up on a seat as kneeling on a footstool, but at least for the children's sake let us not neglect the symbolic expression of our reverence, and let us train in reverent action the young embodied spirits to whom action is no trivial thing.

To the children the way minister and people comport themselves in action and in posture is not insignificant. I fancy they could teach us a thing or two if we explained to them what we intended to express and left them to embody that intention in what seemed to them a fitting expression. Supposing, for instance, they had had no experience of the handing round of the bag or plate, and we told them that at one point in a service we present our gifts of money as an offering to our heavenly Father for use in His service, and then asked them to say how they would make this happy, thankful offering, I wonder what reply we should get? Do you think it would occur to one of them to suggest that we passed round a bag and then that someone should go and dump the bag on the communion table?

I have thrown a doubt on the propriety of the children's address as it is commonly found in Free Church services. To do that is not to claim—on the face of it a ridiculous claim—that it is never either legitimate or useful to address words to the children in a service which is not specifically a children's service. What I do claim is that it is not legitimate unless the address forms an integral part of the living unity of the service as a whole, because where it breaks that unity it is doing violence to that sacred Act to participate in which we come to church, and such violence can profit neither grown-ups nor children.

Before we leave this theme notice should be taken of two arguments which have been adduced in favour of the retention of the children's address, curious arguments, because they are not related to the interests of the children.

It is frequently said : ' It would be a serious mistake to abolish the children's address, since many grown-ups find it much more helpful than the sermon, which is often above their heads.' What reply is there to that ?   Well, if the statement is made to a minister by one of his people, the reply surely is obvious, and it can be made without words : he should go home with the fixed determination that next Sunday he will preach a sermon which shall be full of meaning to the humblest member of his congregation. We are failing in our duty if we are preaching sermons which contain no food for simple Christians whose minds do not run to learning and high argument.

The other argument was put to me by a minister for whose judgement and for whose practical alertness to religious realities I have a very high regard. He said that he often finds the children's address a useful means of saying indirectly to the adults things which need to be said but which would cause embarrassment if said directly. He added that there was no subterfuge involved in this. The senior folk understand perfectly well what he is at and are grateful for this mode of approach. It may be assumed, with this particular minister at all events, that what is thus given for the benefit of the grown-ups is also appropriate, in perhaps a somewhat different way, for the children.

It is possible for an address of this latter kind to take its place as part of a unified and logically articulated rite. Where, however, it can be introduced only by violating this principle of unity, there it is illegitimate, and some other mode of conveying the required instruction or admonition ought to be found.

x

We return to the Anglican Office. After the Second Lesson there is sung (or said) the hymn in Luke i. known as *Benedictus*. When this passage occurs in the Lessons or the Gospel for the day then Psalm c., *Jubilate Deo*, is substituted. Both the *Benedictus* and the *Jubilate* are concluded with the doxology.

The corresponding place in a Free Church Service is commonly filled by a modern hymn.

Next in the Anglican Office is recited by minister and people standing the Apostles' Creed or, on specific occasions, what is known as the Athanasian Creed.

The uninstructed Free Churchman, and with him the man in the street who is not a church-

man of any description, thinks that a creed is
recited in church that the congregation shall
testify to its orthodoxy. In this he is quite
mistaken. Creeds have been put to various
uses, and to serve as a touchstone of orthodoxy
is undoubtedly one of them, but it is not their
liturgical use. The recitation of a creed in a
liturgical service is meant to be an act of prayer,
of worship. Luther was not introducing a
novel idea when, retaining the so-called Nicene
Creed in his ' formula missae " of 1523, he
described it as ' sacrificium laudis '.* At least
up till the 12th century the Creed was absent
from the Roman Mass, and when it came to be
inserted it was for purposes of worship and not
in the interests of correct opinion. ' The
Catholic Church ', writes the Protestant authority
Dr. Will, ' has always conceived the Creed as an
act of adoration.' †

It should not be difficult to see that a solemn
profession of faith may constitute a great act of
corporate worship. The worshippers with one
voice glorify God in proclaiming Him as their
Creator and as the Author and Accomplisher of
man's salvation, and in this act, which is at once
a profession of a common assurance and a
thanksgiving, the bonds are strengthened which

* Vid. Will, *Le Culte*, Vol. I., p. 278.
† ibid., p. 279.

bind them together in the unity of the family of God.

When this liturgical usage of a creed is understood, it is easy to see the force of Dr. Anderson Scott's claim that the " Great Prayer " in a Free Church service takes the place of the Creed not only sequentially but also spiritually. If it is led as it should be it becomes a ' great Confession of Faith ', ' conceived and uttered in the name of the Church ' worshipping in a particular place, and ' also, in a sense, in the name of the Universal Church of God '.* Dr. Anderson Scott holds that this prayer has considerable advantages over a creed : its language is scriptural and familiar and not that of a remote philosophy; it is adaptable to present conditions ; it does not ignore the ethical implications of the relation to God which is proclaimed ; and moreover, ' the great facts of redemption are presented not in the form of propositions, but in relation to persons who by faith have apprehended them, and through obedience are prepared to give them a place in their lives.' †

Obviously the ' Great Prayer ' is not a creed, although it implies a creed, and the inference seems to be that it is better to express your creed by implication than by attempting to

* Vid. C. Anderson Scott, op. cit., p. 58 f.
† ibid., p. 59.

state it simply and directly. Is this true? I think it is true, if by a creed is meant a statement in metaphysical terms of what is believed about God. Such a statement will not truly be understood by those untrained in the philosophical dialect employed, and for those who are versed in the terminology it invites questionings, reservations, and objections. But a creed—a statement of belief about God—need not be set out in metaphysical terms; it may use the language, not of philosophy, but of religion, and scriptural language is supremely the language of religion. Will it be maintained that the Christian Religion has no specific belief about God? Such a claim is surely preposterous. And yet, if its votaries are asked to state in religious terms what their belief is, must they remain dumb? The Church of Christ has come to a pretty pass if they must.

For all that Dr. Anderson Scott says, the ' Great Prayer ' is not a wholly adequate substitute for a united profession of Faith. Its psychological orientation is different. There is not the same focus of attention on the great verities of the faith which obtains when the congregation with united voice gives vocal expression in religious terms to the glorious truths of the faith most surely believed. This latter exercise is not one which should be repeated too often, but practised occasionally it may be an impressive act of worship and a powerful means of grace.

There should be no difficulty in finding a Confession which fulfils the requirements. For instance, it is hard to believe that anyone who calls himself a Christian would feel a scruple about joining in the New Testament Confession of Faith to be found in the Seventh Order of Service in Dr. Orchard's *Divine Service*.

XI

At Mattins after the Creed the minister gives the ancient salutation ' The Lord be with you ', to which the people respond, ' And with thy spirit '. Then the minister says, ' Let us pray ', and there follow the ' Lord, have mercy upon us ' &c., the Lord's Prayer, suffrages consisting of versicles and responses, and three collects— the collect for the day, the collect for peace, and the collect for grace. Next comes, ' in Quires and Places where they sing ', the Anthem, and after that five prayers (for the King's Majesty, for the Royal Family, for the clergy and people, the so-called Prayer of St. Chrysostom, and the Grace) or the Litany together with the last two of the five prayers. This completes the Office of Morning Prayer.

o 209

If we follow Dr. Anderson Scott in holding that the Creed is represented in the Free Church ' Great Prayer ', then we shall say that this prayer corresponds to the closing section of Mattins from the Creed onwards, excluding the anthem and the Grace, which latter commonly concludes the Free Church Service.

On Sunday mornings in a parish church there is usually a sermon. This and the hymns which precede and follow it do not belong properly to the Office, as we have seen. In the Prayer Book it is in the Communion Service that provision for a sermon is made. Its place falls in that part of the Service which is sometimes distinguished as the ' ante-communion '. Whether the position of the sermon in an Anglican morning service is a relic of the days when it was customary to proceed to the Communion after Mattins —whether, that is, historically a normal Sunday morning Service is a truncated form of the double service—or whether the position is simply the inevitable one, which was found because of a demand for preaching quite apart from any connexion with the Communion Service —this is a question difficult to decide. It is obvious, at least, that, since a sermon was not provided for in the Office, the only place for it was outside, either before the Office (which is plainly inappropriate) or after it.

Prayer the Characteristic of a Whole Service

These matters are not merely of academic interest. It is of practical moment to appreciate that, whichever way the question posed is answered, it is not for psychological or dramatic reasons that the sermon comes at the end of Anglican Morning or Evening Prayer. In an ordinary Nonconformist Service it has a similar position. Is that because the position is intrinsically the most fitting one, or is it because of the influence of Anglican practice? The former is commonly assumed, but with doubtful justice. In this respect, as will be argued in the next chapter, there is much to be said for a return to Calvin's model.

Chapter VIII

The Architecture of a Service

I

FEW are the people who will come to church regularly if the services are not interesting —interesting to them, in the sense that they capture and hold their attention for an hour. Our power of volitional attention—attention by force of will to something which does not capture us so that we are interested—is extremely limited. Doubtless we are constantly called upon to use it, and the exercise is necessary to any strength of mind and character; but, to take a motor-car analogy, it is only a ' self-starter ', and we cannot accomplish a journey on it. Unless our volitional attention passes over into spontaneous attention we shall be unable to progress more than a yard or so. Often, when the engine is cold, we must have repeated recourse to the self-starter, but we cannot run on it, and no effective progress is possible until we have warmed to our subject, that is, until our subject has laid hold of our attention.

The Architecture of a Service

All of us have to undergo the discipline of drudgery. Tasks have to be undertaken, not because we are interested in them, but because their performance is in our interests. They are not attractive, but the interest which our performance of them subserves enables us to apply ourselves to them and to find in them a derivative interest sufficient to carry us through. They are not satisfying ends in themselves. That which holds us to them is far more an extrinsic interest then an intrinsic one.

From what has been said earlier in this book about the nature of worship it follows that a service of worship fails in its purpose if it becomes a task of this kind, for true worship does not look beyond itself for a satisfaction. The feeling of the worshipper is : ' It is good for us to be here '. A service, then, must be such as to command spontaneous attention, at least from those whose minds are functioning calmly.*

To be interesting is not, of course, enough ; the service must be interesting in respect of the purpose which it seeks to accomplish. Many attempts to institute ' brighter ' services forget

* Cf. B. H. Streeter, *Concerning Prayer*, p. 263 : ' There is something to be said for the view that it is good for young people occasionally to submit to being bored; there is nothing to be said for the widespread practice of using church services for this purpose. To do so is to kill that instinct of spontaneity which is the very essence of worship.'

this. They hope to draw a congregation by providing an extraneous interest, as an audience is inveigled to a political meeting by cock-shies and dancing on the lawn. It is determined to have plenty of good rousing hymns, by which is meant any hymns which will go with a swing—it matters not what the words are so long as they have some semblance of piety; it matters not at all how meretricious the tunes. Then there will be a ' sacred solo ', preferably sung by a lady who has assumed the title of ' madame '; and naturally the choir must ' render ', and in proof that it is ' rendering ' properly the choir-master will stand on the seat of a front pew, posteriorwise to the congregation, and, baton in hand, will wave his arms and tap his desk. Judiciously interspersed between the items of this entertainment are a short Scripture reading, a short prayer—perhaps two short prayers— and a short, brisk address on some arresting topic.

By means such as these our chapels may be made attractive to some who would not other-wise be attracted by them—though decreas-ingly, one would suppose, since the entertain-ment and the religion can be held at less trouble and in greater variety ' on the wireless '. But what has been gained? The propagation of a little religion perhaps, but hardly the introduction of outsiders to corporate worship and communion. The ' service ' in being made up so as to attract has ceased to be a genuine service. What success it achieves does not belong to its proper sphere; the object which would justify the enterprise is not gained. Therein is exhibited the futility of such methods. Distressing as they are to people more advanced in culture, they should be welcomed and encouraged by them if they attained their purpose; but that they do not, and cannot. A service must hold the attention by its own inherent interest. Truly it should be bright, but with the brightness proper to it, namely that which is derived from the *illuminatio dominica*. Its task is to serve as a medium for this Light, and to this end every part should contribute.

Bearing in mind, then, that a service must be interesting in what is essential to it, let us consider what is required of its fashioning if it is to command spontaneous attention.

II

The first demand which calls for notice is that in thought, word, and symbol a service should be in touch with the experience of the particular congregation met for worship. That does not mean that it should keep on the dead level of that experience. What could be more dull and unprofitable? It does mean, however, that it must meet the people at the point of their interest in spiritual things in terms intelligible to them. This, no doubt, would be accepted as a truism of the sermon, but it applies equally to the prayers and, indeed, all the elements of a service. Not even if you are a Cranmer can you construct a service adequate to the needs of all congregations at all times.

God can speak to us only in terms suited to our capacity to receive; we can speak to him meaningfully only in terms that are clearly related to our experience. This intelligibility must mark those features of a service which represent God's word, and this note of actuality must dominate the part which represents man's word. A service ideally adapted to the requirements of an intellectually and spiritually cultivated congregation is not likely to be suitable without modification for a small country chapel containing, maybe, a handful of simple folk whose horizons are more restricted.*

* Let it not be supposed from this example that I equate intellectual and spiritual cultivation.

The Architecture of a Service

Adaptation is necessary not only because churches differ in spiritual maturity, but also because they differ in 'cultural' background. I refer here not exactly to the difference we mean by 'educated' and 'uneducated', but rather to a distinction like that between an educated Indian and an educated Englishman.

Our fathers in the ministry had an advantage over us in that they had at their disposal a symbolic language, incomparably rich in religious significance, which could be relied upon to find a responsive echo in the hearts of their congregations. It was a language derived from the words, the phrases, the names, and the stories of the Bible. To many congregations in these present days of our Biblical ignorance that language is meaningless. To employ it for these is to court first inattention, and next empty chapels; and yet, not to employ it where it is understood, is as foolish as to present a poetic diet of Felicia Hemans to people who could savour and digest William Shakespeare.

I remember once attending a service in a Congregational chapel with an undergraduate friend—a man of broad culture for his age and of great promise, alas! never to be fulfilled in this world, thanks to the war. In the course of the service we sang Robert Robinson's fine

hymn beginning, ' Come, Thou Fount of every
blessing '. When we reached the lines

> ' Here I raise mine Ebenezer ;
> Hither, by Thy help, I'm come,'

my companion whispered to me : ' What is my
Ebenezer ? I'd gladly raise it if I knew what it
was.' To him the expression was merely funny,
and consequently it was not conducive to
worship; and yet to one who knew and loved
his Old Testament in the manner of a Puritan
it would be of magic power. ' Here I raise
mine Ebenezer ' : the line is charged with
significance expressive of worship and moving
to worship. In a flash the writer gives vivid
expression to his thanksgiving for present help,
creates a sense of God the ever-ready deliverer
down the centuries of history, and links his
experience with that of the faithful through the
ages. Attempt to draw out all the meaning of
the line in plain prose, and it would take at
least a sermon ; and at the end you would have
lost much of the stimulating effect of the chord
by your analysis of the harmonies.

Mr. E. C. Ratcliff objects to the permissive
uses (worst of all the sanction of extemporaneous
prayer after the conclusion of the Offices or of
any other service) ' at the discretion of the

minister ' allowed by the proposed Prayer Book revision of 1927–28. They would have opened the door, he complains, ' to all the confusions of ministerial idiosyncrasy and experiment from which the fixed Liturgy of the Book of Common Prayer at its last revision was intended as a safeguard '. ' That the confusions ', he proceeds, ' would have been supported or desired by Parochial Church Councils is neither a recommendation nor a mitigation of an evil. . . . The principle of one Use for the whole realm was to have been exchanged for that of *Quot ecclesiae tot liturgiae.*' *

' Ministerial idiosyncrasy ' : how destructive of corporate worship that can be the Nonconformist, to his cost, knows better than any man, but he will go on maintaining that ministerial ' discretion ' must be allowed by a living church whose offices of worship are to be adequate to the many varied needs of our modern complex civilization. Even the principle, ' every local church its own Use ', is not elastic enough. The demand made by ordinary men and women for what is called ' reality ' in a service requires the wider principle, ' every occasion of public worship its own

* *Liturgy and Worship*, ed. by W. K. Lowther Clarke, p. 287.

Use '. This principle, it may be admitted, is more bad than good if it stands by itself. It must be brought into harmony with other principles no less important—those relating to order and content, the element of familiarity, and so on. Rightly interpreted, however, it leads, not to chaotic anarchy, but to a living variety in an essential unity of practice.

Some Anglican theological colleges have been criticized derisively in the past on the ground that a larger proportion of the pitifully short time given to the training of ordinands was devoted to matters of ritual and devotional practice than to theology. We need not discuss here the justice of such criticism. For Free Churchmen it is more profitable to look to our own shortcomings, and to realize that with our liturgical freedom there is even greater need for training in these things than there is for our Anglican brothers with their fixed liturgy and their authoritative rubrics. And what is the record of our theological colleges in this respect? Are they not in large measure responsible for the ministerial idiosyncrasies which blight so many churches?

To resume : in order to be interesting a service must be in vital touch with the experience of the particular congregation. Also, to hold

the attention it must have variety and movement within a dramatically unified whole.

III

We have seen earlier that the structure of a
service should be such as best to facilitate both
expression and *creation*—the expression of the
religious consciousness of the group, and the
creation of a deeper apprehension of God. If
words—the fruit of lips which make confession
to Jesus' name (Heb. xiii. 15)—are the media
of our sacrifice, they are also the sacramental
means of God speaking to us. Communion is
the to and fro commerce between God and his
human child. It cannot be urged too strongly
that a public office of worship can only achieve
its end by the *formal representation* of this
double movement. Its task is to give formal
embodiment to man's word to God and to God's
word to man. Uttered words are to be the
sacraments whereby living communion is in-
augurated and sustained. As we saw when
examining a typical service, the whole should
be characterized by the alternating rhythm of
this double movement.

A service must express the worship which it
is in the hearts of the worshippers to offer.

This business of expression is not easy. Many folk have not the art to set out that which is struggling in their hearts for expression, and it is a real liberation for them when the service says more or less adequately what they are too inarticulate to say for themselves. This consideration alone should make us realize that the effective conduct of public worship finds its closest analogy in a work of art. A service is required to perform a task similar to that which the poet performs for us when he clothes in fitting words some sentiment which we cherish, and in thus objectifying it beautifully both strengthens and clarifies the sentiment and also releases that inner tension which always exists where strong feeling is unable to find expression.

But, as I have said, the aim of a service is also to create. The means of creation is the *re-presentation of the fundamental Christian verities* which have been borne witness to by many generations of Christian men. This representation is a constituent of almost every phase of a service. It is (or should be) present in varying degree in Scripture, prayers, hymns, and sermon.

Let me illustrate what I mean by creative re-presentation, and how it and expression are interrelated.

The Architecture of a Service

We will take the beautiful morning prayer :

' O Lord, our heavenly Father, Almighty and everlasting God, who hast safely brought us to the beginning of this day ; defend us in the same with thy mighty power, and grant that this day we fall into no sin, neither run into any kind of danger ; but that all our doings may be ordered by thy governance, to do always that is righteous in thy sight ; through Jesus Christ our Lord.'

There are many things to observe in this brief prayer. Notice especially the following. It is a petition, but it fixes the attention much more upon God than upon our needy selves. Moreover, in it we not only ask, but we are provided with the divine answer, which will be brought to the test of experience if we receive it. We ask for things requisite and necessary as well for the body as for the soul, and we do more : we set forth God's most worthy praise, and we hear his most holy word. Through the symbolism of words we have re-presented before us Him whom the generations of Christ's folk have worshipped in adoring dependence and filial trust : the Lord to whom we have sworn fealty, the heavenly Father on whom we depend and who cares for us, his power as a very present help, his demand for righteousness as summed up in personal terms in Jesus Christ.

' O Lord, our heavenly Father, Almighty and everlasting God, who hast safely brought us to the beginning of this day ' : the mists which obscure for us the eternal Father of our spirits begin to roll away; we begin to be conscious of the Presence—not a vague numinous we-know-not-what, but One who may be apprehended (though never comprehended) with positive, meaningful attributes. We pass on to petition, and it is not now a desperate cry into the void; it is a petition which goes out to meet its answer, so that it has scarcely escaped our lips before the divine response is given in such wise as to make the request seem almost superfluous : ' defend us in the same—with thy mighty power.' We have come into the relationship of communion. For us God has become the supreme, pressing reality, and our very petitions are regulated by this. ' Grant that this day we fall into no sin . . . that all our doings may be ordered by *thy* governance, to do always that is righteous in *thy* sight.'

I daresay it may be thought that I am here attributing more power to a form of words than any mere words are capable of mediating, but that would be due to a misunderstanding. I am not maintaining that this prayer can be relied upon always and for all men to manifest the efficacy which I suggest it possesses potentially. There is no magic formula guaranteed to bring us into the presence of God and into communion with him. We cannot say when the kindling of the Spirit will take place. The whole service must be devised to make ready the most favourable conditions. Rather, this prayer illustrates the rhythm which must pulse through a service if it is to achieve its end, communion with God. There must be the constant interplay between the outgoing movement of the worshippers towards God in desire, contrition, thanksgiving, &c. and their responsiveness to him as he meets them, answering or forestalling, in his most holy word. It will not be a dull, monotonous alternation, but the two movements Godward and manward will succeed one another and answer one another in rich and stimulating variety like subject and counter-subject in a fugue.

We may reiterate, then, that in respect to its form a service should be a symbolical representation of communion, that through the sacramental use of words it may become for the worshippers the entrance to communion indeed.

IV

Here it will be valuable to draw a distinction between words used as sacraments and words used as an objectification of an inner movement of spirit. In concrete instances the distinction is rarely absolute, yet it is important, because failure to draw it is frequently responsible for shortcomings in the conduct of a service. An illustration will, perhaps, make clear my meaning.

Suppose that I retire to my room for prayer. There I may enter into simple, spontaneous converse with God. That is the highest, richest kind of private prayer. In so far as words are used they are an objectification of an inner movement of spirit—which means that, however valuable their utterance may be, they are not absolutely *necessary*. It may be, however, that communion does not come easily, and in order to achieve it I have recourse to the words of another, reading them from a book or repeating them from memory. Here the words are used as sacraments. It is better not to need crutches, but, as has been said, ' only those who add folly to lameness despise crutches.' *

Now let me leave my room and walk over to

* Vid. B. A. Brasnett, *The Infinity of God*, p. 11.

226

the chapel to lead the worshippers in prayer. If I am fitly prepared in spirit I may be able to pray on their behalf in such wise that the words uttered are for me but the making audible of an inner movement of spirit. It is natural for me to feel that this is the truest, most spiritual way of prayer in public, for its superiority is for me the superiority of spontaneous talk with God over the prayers which lean on human aid. But I must be careful not to be carried away by my own feeling here, as I am in danger of being carried away if I forget one fact, the fact, namely, that however spontaneous the words uttered may be for me, at the highest they are, and can only be, sacramental for the congregation. That is to say, the spoken word in public prayer serves the purpose for the congregation which the book serves for me in private prayer. Moreover, it is a serious mistake for me to assume that the objectification of my communion with God is an effective sacrament of communion for the congregation, even though it is the needs of the congregation which are the burden of my soul in prayer. It may be or it may not be; but my feeling of direct communion is no criterion of whether it is or not.

Many readers will have had experience of

ministers to overhear whose prayers from the pulpit was a true sacrament of communion— rare souls, with a rare gift. We deceive ourselves, however, if we conclude from such experience that, in order that our words may be sacramental, all we have to do is to pray genuinely and with consecration. It is a cardinal error.

We Free Churchmen talk (sometimes, psychologists would tell us, with suspicious warmth) about our precious heritage of *ex tempore* prayer. Precious truly it is, and we should hold it in trust to preserve and to pass on. But let us be clear what we mean by it, and what constitutes its preciousness. Surely it is precious because, and only because, it implies the liberty (and with the liberty the duty) *to make the prayers correspond to the realities of time and place in which the worshippers have their being, and to reify those prayers in no matter what words so long as they be the most effective available for their sacramental use.*

If, on the other hand, we mean by *ex tempore* prayer, prayer which is unpremeditated, or (more probably, but less honestly) which has the appearance of being unpremeditated, then our heritage is not our treasure but our bane. Such a view presupposes a pneumatic type of religion which does not belong to us, and with which our services as a whole simply cannot be reconciled.

Lord Cockburn said that he had never known a truly extemporary preacher. In the sense in which he used the phrase, most of us could say that we have never known a truly extemporary pray-er. This lack does not trouble us, because we do not believe in the value of the kind of extemporizing implied. In principle we do not believe in it, but can we sincerely say that in practice we never make shift to seem to believe in it?

v

I have drawn attention to the sacramental use of words in public worship. It must not be forgotten that they are spoken words, and therefore that their sacramental potency is notably dependent upon the manner in which they are uttered. That they may be conducive to living communion they must be right words and rightly spoken. Most important of all is that the accent of reality should be in the speaking. No artifice can successfully simulate this. There is but one way to achieve it : the speaker must have his own heart in what he is saying, meaning it sincerely and devoutly. This must be a ruling principle; and yet all the same the speaking requires art.

It is supremely important that the minister should mean what he says, but plainly that will not be enough if he does not articulate his words audibly. Now even with successful audibility we have already introduced at least a modicum of art; but more is needed. If words are to have their full force they must be stressed correctly according to their importance and according to the context in which they are set. The right use of stress and intonation is of very high value in keeping alive the hearer's interest, and so maintaining attention. Further, emphasis and intonation must be subservient to the occasion of speech. There is a quietness necessary for communion with God. This quietness must pervade the spoken prayers in public worship, which means that the requisite audibility, emphasis, and variety of intonation must be effected within the range of subdued speech. It is impossible to adore if you are being bawled at; it is difficult to be conscious of the gracious Father's presence if He is being harangued.

Again, the question of *tempo* has to be considered. I have urged in this book that our aim should be *common* prayer. To this end the prayers must be spoken at a pace which enables the worshippers to make them their own, and it would seem evident that that pace must be slower if they do not know what is coming than if they do. We must remember, however, that it is easy to be too slow—exasperatingly slow. Attention will quickly wander where the holding of it involves strain, and it is difficult to say which is the more tiring, to attempt to follow words at too high or too low a speed. The task of finding the comfortable mean between these extremes is a delicate one. When it is found, it will be a speed admitting of gradations. This was in fact implied in what I said about emphasis, because pace as well as stress is a factor in emphasis.

Mr. T. L. Harris out of ' experience gained from listening to many services well and ill rendered ' makes the following suggestions for liturgical reading (they are equally applicable to free utterance). ' The most sacred and solemn words should be read distinctly but with as low a voice as is consistent with its being heard. . . . The joyful words should be given a more vigorous and rather more rapid expression. Words of penitence are naturally said softly and rather rapidly—listen to any child confess its faults to its mother.' * These

* Thomas L. Harris, *Christian Public Worship*, p. 154. In the context Mr. Harris is writing of Holy Communion.

suggestions illustrate what I mean by gradations within the normal speed.

What this normal speed should be will vary, as we have seen, according to circumstances. The recognition of this truth leads to an important observation : the amount of ground covered should be in proportion to the rapidity of speech; that is to say, if the pace has to be slow, the service must not be lengthened in order to include all the themes which a greater speed would allow in a given time. We must cut our coat according to our cloth, and our 'cloth' in this application is the time which can be allotted to a whole service—as a prudent general rule, an hour. True corporate prayer makes exacting demands on the worshippers; brevity is imperative by reason of its intensity. Let the prayers be long in length as well as leisurely in pace, and attention will be dissipated almost at the outset.

Not only will the subjects for petition and intercession be limited by the amount of time available for prayer in a service, but the periods of prayer within the service will be short, and their themes unified, in the interests of concentration. The long 'omnibus' prayer (which has hardly yet ceased to be characteristic of the Free Church ritual) cannot be a means of full common prayer without a psychological miracle.

The Architecture of a Service

Canon Streeter, with characteristic perspicuity, has said the sane word on this subject, and I make free to quote from it :

' If a service is to be conducted in such a way as to make it possible for all to take part in it *up to the maximum of their capacity*, its guiding principle should be " one thing at a time "; and those parts of worship which demand the greatest concentration should be broken up by intervals. That is to say, confession, thanksgiving, petition for personal needs, and intercession for others, should not be combined in one long supplication, they should be divided from one another by the other and less exacting elements in the service, such as hymns or Scripture reading. And not only that, but whenever in any of these divisions the congregation is to be invited to pass from one subject to another the change ought not to be sudden, unexpected or hurried. The minister knows beforehand what is to be the next subject of confession or thanksgiving or the next petition, but the mind of the congregation (which in any case moves more slowly than that of an individual) should have notice in advance, and time given for the change.' *

There must be art in the ordering of a service

* *Concerning Prayer*, p. 286 f. Canon Streeter's whole essay on Worship in this book should be consulted.

and (to return to our consideration of speech) art in the choice of words and art in the speaking of them. If we are honest we must accept this. It should not cause misgiving, when we remember the paradox that good art is that which is most ' natural '. Words must be articulated properly ; and that means they must be clearly audible in terms of their ordinary correct pronunciation, and not that voice should be given to vowels or consonants which are mute in everyday speech nor that syllables should be mouthed artificially. Again, pace and stress must be such as to give to a sentence fullest life and intelligibility ; and this will never be where emphasis is forced. These things demand care and thought and practice. Only self-conceit, not piety, will permit us to think otherwise. But the ground-principle of this art is sincerity : sincerity of word, sincerity of vocal utterance. Wherefore let us ask as a boon of heaven that our ' natural ' voice be not a ' parsonic ' one.

VI

In order to maintain interest a service needs to be an organic unity rhythmical and varied in its parts. It is not enough that it should consist of unrelated, or loosely related, numbers, however admirable they may be in themselves. The service as a whole must have shape and meaning. Anthologies have their value, but they are not meant to be read continuously. To use them thus is to court a feeling of restlessness and frustration. An anthological service produces a similar effect.

The reader will see that there is an æsthetic law involved here. It is sufficient for us, however, to note the fact without stopping to investigate the theory. A service to be interesting and satisfying must constitute a living whole. When it fails to observe the principles of unity and organic continuity the worshippers suffer from a malaise which is not the less depressing because few of them have the faintest notion of its cause.

In view of the various functions which we have seen a service has to perform, a psychologically sound order would appear to be one which begins with the revelation of God, followed successively by an opportunity for contemplation of that which has been revealed, by the corporate act of self-offering to God, and by corporate concern for the brethren and for the world in the power of the experience of God which has been vouchsafed. A service ordered in this manner will have three main phases of unequal length, which, borrowing from the story of the Transfiguration, we may label, (1) the Opening of the Heavens, (2) the Waiting in the Presence on the Mountain Top, and (3) the Descent to the Plain.*

There is involved in this scheme a slight redistribution of the elements which customarily go to make up a Free Church service, and also one addition. The chief changes are that the sermon, the preaching of the Gospel, will take its place as the culmination of the first, and longest, division of the service; that an opportunity for silent worship is provided at the point of the service where the summit of vision has been reached; and that the vows of consecration, the intercessions, and the offertory will take their natural place in the final division as the active response of the worshippers to the vision they have had, and as linking their experience of God to the ordinary active concerns and duties and relationships of everyday life.

Exception will at once be taken by some to this plan on the ground that the sermon is relegated to a subordinate position; but further

* I fancy I am indebted to the suggestion of another for this nomenclature, but, if so, I cannot lay my hand on the reference and acknowledge the source of my indebtedness.

reflexion will, I hope, reveal to objectors that the position is not one of subordination but of far greater power. It gives the message much more chance to be digested by the worshippers and to be transmuted into vital practical activity, and I urge it for spiritual and psychological reasons. Incidentally, Puritans need hardly fear a change as too revolutionary which marks a reversion to the practice of John Calvin. One *caveat* must be introduced, however. A sermon can fittingly hold this changed position only when it is a true ' elevation of the Host ', that is, only when it is a true setting forth of God in Christ in such wise as to evoke worship. If this condition is to be observed it means death to the church posters with their flagrant attempts to make sermon-title and preacher as alluring as film and film-star; but the funeral will surely be dry-eyed and triumphant.

An outline of a service ordered on the principles we have considered may be helpful. It is necessary to insist, however, that what is here given is simply an illustration of how the principles may be applied to a service without doing great violence to traditional ways. In these things improvements have to come slowly, or they are not improvements; and I bear in mind Canon Streeter's wise saying that ' no new or revised " Order of Service " . . . can be even tolerably good unless it is organically related to and a natural development of the custom and practice of the past.' * The following, then, claims no finality or perfection.

An Order of Service.†

OPENING OF THE HEAVENS

1. Call to worship.
2. (a) A setting forth of God's glory; (b) the response of the congregation.

 Note : (a) may take the form either of sentences from Scripture or of a prayer, and (b) may fittingly be a hymn of praise. Alternatively (a) and (b) may be combined in a hymn. The hymns should be an integral part of the service, not mere padding and emotion-raising stuff, and what is said in a hymn should not need to be said again in a prayer.

3. (a) Prayer of confession and for forgiveness. It will be suitable if this is introduced by sentences awakening the worshippers to

* *Concerning Prayer*, p. 290.

† Cf. Will, op. cit., Vol. I., p. 435; also Otto, *Zur Erneuerung und Ausgestaltung des Gottesdienstes*, pp. 59 ff. My obligation to these will be obvious, although the Order given differs in many respects from both.

God's law, his holiness, &c., and it should close with a statement of his promise of grace.

(*b*) The response of the congregation in a hymn of thanksgiving or some other act of praise.

4. (*a*) O.T. Lesson.

(*b*) Response in hymn, psalm, or canticle.

5. (*a*) N.T. Lesson.

(*b*) Response in hymn, psalm, canticle, or gloria.

6. The Sermon.

WAITING ON THE MOUNTAIN TOP

7. Silence (the congregation in the attitude of prayer).

Note : Given the right organist and a suitable instrument the silence may be preceded by a brief interlude on the organ and/or, given a congregation which would understand, the Sursum Corda and the Sanctus (in English of course).

DESCENT TO THE PLAIN

8. (*a*) A short prayer of consecration, and possibly (*b*) a hymn. Or simply a hymn of consecration.

9. The Notices.
10. Intercession (which should conclude with an affirmation of God's love).
11. The Offertory. This ought to be a great act of Christian solidarity, and it demands a dignified, however simple, ceremonial.
12. Closing Hymn.
13. Benediction.

It ought not to be necessary to point out that the Blessing should be the final act of the service. Unfortunately in many chapels it is followed in the evening service by a monstrosity called a Vesper. However beautiful this Vesper might be in itself it is quite intolerable in the place allotted to it; and of the most popular one all that can be said is that the maudlin sentimentality of the words is equalled by the maudlin sentimentality of the tune.*

The foregoing Order is intended to illustrate what should be the rhythm and shape of an ordinary service. It is patient of considerable modification in detail without destroying either the one or the other.

* Words and tune referred to may be found in *Let us Pray*, compiled by C. S. Horne and T. H. Darlow, p. 93 f. In mitigation of the evil it must be said that these compilers did at least place the Benediction *after* the Vesper.

The Architecture of a Service

It is generally agreed that the use of hymns has become stereotyped to an extent very destructive of their value. New life would be given to many of them if their verses, or parts of their verses, were employed as responses to suitable Scripture readings. For instance, Milton's ' How lovely are Thy dwellings fair ' may be taken verse by verse in response to appropriate passages of Scripture with stimulating effect. The minister reads a short passage leading up appropriately to the first verse, which is then sung by the congregation; then another leading to the second verse, and so on. Or again, the minister may take a series of short readings illustrative of the life and work of Jesus to each of which the congregation sings in response the words ' O come let us adore him, Christ the Lord ' from *Adeste Fideles*. The method can be adapted in a variety of ways. It is conducive to living, active corporate worship, and it can be made of real interest to the children. Moreover, although it may be novel, it is nevertheless in harmony with Free Church tradition.

I

THE Communion Service is the Service *par
excellence* of the Christian Church. That is
a statement of history. This Service, however
elaborated, however simplified, involves some
sort of re-enactment of what happened once
when the intimate disciples of Jesus were met
together for the last time in the bodily as well
as spiritual presence of their Master—a supreme
occasion in history, an occasion which no
Christian can let his mind rest upon without
feeling the stirrings of awe. Ever since then in
unbroken continuity the Church has always
done this, and however formal and mechanical
the doing of it may have at times become,
always before long the vital religious significance
of the enactment has re-emerged—not perhaps
in its fullness, yet none the less with power—so
that men have found in it the epitome of their
faith.

To say that the Church has always observed

244

this rite is not to say that the whole of the Church has always done so : that would be palpably false. What is true is that the great main streams of Church tradition have always been faithful to it, that the tradition has been unbroken from the very beginning, and that the profoundest religious experiences of generations of Christians have been intimately bound up with it.

Thus for a local church or congregation to give up the ' breaking of bread ' simply because the rite does not appeal to it is to be culpably schismatic, for it is to cut itself loose from one of the bonds which bind it most closely to the great Church. There may be grave reasons in the interests of the great Church for such a schism, as there are, no doubt, in the minds of the Quakers. That is a different matter; principle is involved, and whether or not the principle is sound, while it is held it demands to be acted upon in the interests of the whole. But where the breaking away has for its motive not principle but whim or fancy, then it shows a blameworthy disregard for Christian solidarity, and an arrogant and ignorant unwillingness to learn from the experience of the wider brotherhood.

This is said, not because the rite is ceasing to

be celebrated in the Free Churches, but because there is a large number of practising Free Church-men who see no value in it, and to some of whom, indeed, it is positively repugnant. Be-fore we consider the reasons for this, however, some defence is required of the claim that neglect of the sacrament may indicate a disregard for Christian solidarity.

II

It will be urged that so far from its being a prime factor making for Christian unity there is nothing more divisive of Christendom than the Communion Service. There is distressing truth in this, truth so obvious as to be in no need of proof. Take an illustration. There are many Anglicans who gladly acknowledge Noncon-formists as their Christian brethren, and who are willing on occasion to worship with them in a Nonconformist chapel, yet who refuse to sit with them at the Lord's table at a Free Church celebration. Again, there are many Anglicans who welcome Nonconformists to Mattins or Evensong (and not as pagans, but as fellow-Christians), but who will not welcome them to the altar. What sense, therefore, is there in saying that a Nonconformist by neglecting to

246

attend Communion in his chapel is taking a course which tends to cut him off from his fellow-Christians of a different order?

There would certainly be no sense in it, except for the fact that the Lord's table is the Lord's table, and that table is not made of wood or stone, nor is it many tables. There is only one Upper Room; there is only one Lord Jesus Christ who hands to his disciples the bread, saying, This is my Body. You did not see me there as you knelt at Mass; I did not see you there as I sat waiting to receive the bread in the ugly little chapel. Yet we have been in the same holy place, preciously familiar to our fellow-Christians from the earliest days; the same words spoken by the same Person have rung in our ears; we have been at the same banquet and have partaken of the same spiritual food. Afterwards we pass in the street and we do not recognize one another as blood-brothers. No, but all unconscious of it we are both engaged on the same family business. Later on, perhaps, circumstances bring us together socially, and we gradually become aware of an affinity which puzzles us. It seems unaccountable, because our points of view on religious and ecclesiastical matters are in many very serious respects irreconcilably opposed.

What is the explanation? Might it not possibly be—remarkable discovery—that we had both been in that Upper Room, not merely as onlookers, but as participants in that supreme enactment of giving and receiving?

The foregoing paragraph will probably be regarded by some readers as sheer sentimentalism. The celebration of the Eucharist at Holy Trinity church is not the same as the celebration of the Lord's Supper at (less holy) Trinity chapel. Agreed; they are not the same, if by ' the same ' we mean ' indistinguishable '. But solemnly to commemorate the Last Supper is the same as solemnly to commemorate the Last Supper, and to feed on the life of the Risen Lord is the same as to feed on the life of the Risen Lord. Doubtless other things may be done wherein church and chapel are at variance, and there may also be differences in the manner of the commemoration and differences of opinion about the mode of communion; but either there is the commemoration or there is not, either there is communion or there is not. Those who have commemorated and communicated have been spiritually in the same place and they have been subject, in that which is essential and vital, to the same experience. *If* they have commemorated—that can be ascertained without much controversy; *if* they have communicated—who is to judge?

At the Lord's table the disunion of Christendom is brought into focus. It is a deplorable truth. Why at that most sacred place? Surely the answer is simple : because that most sacred place *is* the focus of the Church. What is deplorable is the disunion of Christians, and how unbearably wrong that is is brought to light at the Lord's table. There the evil nature of disunion is made manifest as nowhere else; there our ' unhappy divisions ' are seen to be not so much unhappy as monstrous.

The dissensions of the Church cannot be healed by abandoning the holy table, unless suicide be regarded as a cure. On the contrary, it is there alone that lies the hope of their healing. The Eucharist, despite all appearances to the contrary, is the sacrament of Christian unity. It is dominical in origin; * it derives its meaning from the double reality of the living Lord and the living brotherhood; it sets forth the central mystery of our common faith; it links us in word and in action with the faithful in all ages; it is the pledge of the

---

* The question whether it is of dominical institution as a perpetual sacrament of the Church involves much larger issues which cannot be treated of here.

communion of saints. The more living and significant it is for us the more aware do we become of the Body of Christ, which is the Church. Even in its divisiveness is the hope of unity, because while it accentuates the cleavages between Christian groups at the same time it shows how intolerably inconsistent with itself are these very divisions.

Unbelievers do not tire of pointing out that no differences are more bitterly maintained than religious differences. A follower of Christ undoubtedly ought to see that this bitterness is wholly reprehensible. Nevertheless the calm observer should draw an inference from it which is hardly hostile to religion itself. People feel most strongly about those things which touch them most intimately. The bitterness (reprehensible as it is) of religious controversy bears witness to the central significance of religion to men; it is, so far as it goes, evidence of religion's inalienable right in life. Similarly the heat of the controversy which has raged round the sacrament of Holy Communion is *prima facie* evidence of the central importance of that sacrament.

The stridency with which a controversialist proclaims his views and the bitterness * with

* N.B. ' bitterness ', not ' severity '. The Lord Jesus was

which he attacks his opponents are, it is true, evidence of his weakness, not of his strength. They mark the precariousness of his hold upon what he is maintaining; yes, but they mark too an inward assurance that there is an issue at stake of vital importance. Saul of Tarsus persecuting the Christians was violently on the wrong side. His violence showed at once his realization of the magnitude of the issue and the measure of the uncertainty in the depth of his soul.

III

I have urged the paradox that the sacrament which is most divisive of Christendom is yet the sacrament of Christian unity. I go further, and say that this sacrament is the touchstone of historic Christianity, by which I mean that, unless the use of names is to be arbitrary and out of relation to their history, whether or not a man is entitled to call himself a Christian depends upon his belief or disbelief in the perpetually present reality of Christ's offering of Himself to His gathered disciples and upon his reception of that gift by faith.

---

on occasion severe, but there is no evidence of his being bitter.

This is not put forward as a new definition of orthodoxy in the sense of what is correct or true opinion in theology, nor is it a judgement of comparative value, as that a bad Christian is better than a good non-Christian theist; it is simply an assertion about the proper use of names. Interpretations vary inevitably, but it is nonsense to talk of interpretations varying unless they are interpretations of the same datum or the same data. Historically the fellowship of the Church was formed on the basis of a new covenant in Christ's blood; historically this fellowship has derived its life and nourishment from feeding on the Bread of Life, which is the living Christ. These fundamental data are embodied and asserted in that rite which the Church has celebrated from the beginning, a rite which has been preservative of the Church's most precious and most distinctive treasure. You may say that it is a delusion that the Lord's death sealed any covenant and that it is an unwarrantable assumption that the Church derives its spiritual vitality from the action of the living Christ, but if you say these things (whether you are right or whether you are wrong) you are opposing the witness of historical Christianity, and your gospel (if you have a gospel) is not the Gospel which the Church has always preached. In the interests of truth it does not seem right to hide a distinction of this kind by covering it with the same name.

The sacrament of the Lord's Supper not only promotes the unity of the Church, it also epitomizes that wherein the Church is, and has always been, one.

I imagine it will be at once objected that I am unchurching such Christian bodies as the Society of Friends and the Salvation Army. To this objection I reply that, if I were, I should be making a very foolish assertion, but I am not.

Let it be repeated, the Lord's table is not made of wood or stone, nor is it many tables. It is ' in heaven ', not ' on earth ', and the food to be received at it is spiritual, not material. It may be symbolically objectified by a material table, and the food may be symbolically objectified by material bread and wine, but it is possible to sit at the table and receive the food without any of these symbolical objectifications, as also it is possible to sit at the material table and partake of the material bread and wine, and yet not to have been at the Lord's table and not to have communicated in truth.

The Quaker who refuses chalice and paten is not thereby excluded from the Upper Room.

His communion may be 'sacramental' in a sense of the phrase akin to the Roman usage where it is applied to the communion of those present at the Mass who do not actually receive the wafer. That may be true enough; and yet, is there not a real danger that by eschewing the 'visible word' he will in time forget the table? The propensity in Quakerism to a mysticism which is not specifically Christian at least suggests this danger.

IV

A very large number of Free Churchmen who attend their chapel on Sundays rarely avail themselves of the sacrament of the Lord's Supper to which as church members and professing Christians they are invited. Why is this?

We may note three common reasons, which may be named briefly (1) rationalism, (2) ignorance, and (3) ministerial incompetence; and we might add a fourth: microbes. Let us take them in turn.

(1) ' In the course of the eighteenth century ', writes Dr. F. J. Powicke of Congregationalism, ' partly as the result of an extreme reaction

254

from everything supposed to be Romish, and partly as the result of a rationalism which destroyed all sense of the mystical in religion, the Congregational Churches forgot, to a great extent, their proper doctrine of the Real Presence. They lapsed into what is often styled, perhaps misstyled, sheer Zwinglianism. The Lord's Supper became merely a memento of the Past, and faith an effort to recall what once had been rather than a realization of what eternally is. This impoverished attitude of mind persisted far into the nineteenth century, and has still many representatives. Reaction toward the older and truer view was set going under the influence of the Evangelical Revival, and has been strengthened in more recent times by stimulus from the Oxford movement.' *

If the service of Holy Communion is regarded simply as a memorial of the Last Supper then the manner in which the rite is conducted to-day—whether Roman, Anglican, or Free Church—is not well adapted to its purpose, and we can hardly be surprised if men and women do not feel it worth while to attend. Neither the Catholic altar nor the Protestant table

* F. J. Powicke on 'The Congregational Churches' in *Evangelical Christianity Its History and Witness*, ed. by W. B. Selbie, p. 106 f. The book was published in 1911.

represents very vividly the circumstances of the
Upper Room, and a tolerably educated man's
historical imagination is likely to be kindled far
more effectively by the reading of the New
Testament accounts of the scene than by the
contemplation of the ritual furniture and the
ritual action which meet the eye in church or
chapel. It is true that the actions of the communicant himself at the Service may help to
stir his imagination, but the value of this is
considerably offset by the lack of verisimilitude
in the scenery. Many who hold the so-called
Zwinglian theory continue to frequent the sacrament in obedience to what they believe to be
the Lord's command. The theory, however,
spells the death of the sacrament once a serious
doubt has been harboured whether that command was to all subsequent generations of
Christians.

(2) There are some Free Churchmen who
object to the Communion Service because, they
say, the notion of eating the flesh and drinking
the blood of Christ is wholly repugnant. It is
indeed revolting, but then it is a notion which
is not entertained by any instructed Protestant,
and it is a notion which manifestly would not
be in the mind of Jesus or in the minds of his
disciples at the Last Supper.

Canon J. S. Bezzant makes this latter point well in discussing St. Paul's account of the institution of the Lord's Supper in 1 Corinthians xi. 23, 24. There are two objections, he says, to any literal interpretation of the words ' This is my body ' and ' This cup is the new covenant in my blood '. ' First, St. Paul, like the Synoptists, represents Jesus as saying " This is my body " when he was still alive in His body of flesh, eating and drinking in the presence of His disciples. A strictly literal interpretation of the second words would involve us in the absurdity that the cup itself, not the wine in it, is the new covenant. Not only so, but the idea of drinking blood would have been repugnant to any Jew. It is therefore as unlikely that the Twelve would have understood, in any literal sense, that the wine was the blood of Jesus, as it is impossible that they could have understood, in any literal sense, the bread to be His body. As the old Covenant was sealed in blood, so a wine-cup was to be the pledge of the new Covenant which was to be sealed with Christ's blood. The wine represents His covenant-blood, for the words suggest no change whatever in the contents of the cup beyond a change of significance or value. Similarly with the words " This is my body." When St. Paul calls the Church " the body of Christ " the phrase is a simile : it is symbolical. If the bread is His body, is it so in any other sense? St. Paul definitely associates both similies. He writes " The bread which we break, is it not a participation in the body of Christ? because one bread, one body, are we, the many ".' *

' Narrow pedantry and unimaginative literalism in exegesis have ever been chief obstacles to the understanding of the mind of Jesus ', writes Canon O. C. Quick.† The words of institution are a good example of language which is misleading to the extent to which its literal significance is pressed, and which is illuminating according to the measure in which force is given to its analogical meaning.

(3) The third reason for neglect of the Lord's Supper I have called ' ministerial incompetence '. I have been present at Communion Services in chapels where the minister apparently had little or no understanding of the purpose of the service.

* *The Modern Churchman*, Vol. XVI, Nos. 6, 7, 8, p. 351 f.

† *The Christian Sacraments*, p. 188. This book is an important contribution to the discussion of sacramental theory, and it would demand detailed consideration if I were making any pretence to a thorough treatment of eucharistic doctrine. The above quotation must not be taken as a clue to the author's main thesis.

The Lord's Supper

The impression conveyed was that here was an ordinance the observance of which tradition demanded, but there was complete ignorance of the parts of which it is traditionally composed, except for the recitation of the words of institution and the actual distribution of the elements, and there seemed to be distressingly little feeling for the sanctity of the occasion.

It is a tradition of the Church (and not only a Protestant tradition) that the sacrament of the Eucharist is associated with the ministry of the Word, and it cannot be too strongly insisted upon. For the moment, however, let us concentrate upon the Communion rite apart from the reading and preaching from which it must not in fact be dissociated.

Without claiming that there should be absolute uniformity either in the structure or in the language of the service we can confidently affirm that there are various acts to be performed which no presiding minister should feel free to omit, and, moreover, that these acts will largely determine the structure of the service if any regard is paid to dramatic unity. They belong to the essential meanings of the rite : the Lord's table to which his disciples are invited, the fellowship meal of the Church which is the body of Christ, the commemoration of the Incarnation, Passion, Resurrection, and Ascension, in the spirit of eucharist or thanksgiving, the communion, the worship with its fundamental characteristic of offering—however divided, however combined, all these constituents should be represented, and appropriate expression given to them whether in utterance, or in silence, or in symbolical action.

The blessed invitation will be given (perhaps best in sentences of Scripture), and for those who respond to it an initial requirement must be satisfied : confession of sin and prayer for pardon, which may fittingly be followed by ' comfortable ' words and a prayer of ' humble access '.

The fellowship of the table must be realized, and that means prayer, and the bearing in mind of the present and the absent and the dear departed of the fellowship, and of the whole church militant on earth and of the great company of witnesses in heaven. In spirit all meet at the table. The heavens are opened. Nor can the faithful gather together forgetful of the world, groaning and travailing : there must be intercession.

The service is a memorial and a eucharist and a supreme act of worship. The mighty acts of God in and through our Lord Jesus Christ are to be celebrated in memorial word with glory and thanksgiving, and expression must be given to the self-oblation of the worshippers.

Central to the whole is the re-enactment of what took place in the Upper Room when the Lord took bread, and, having given thanks, brake it, and said, Take, eat, this is my body, and when He took the cup, saying, This cup is the new covenant in my blood. And here it must be said that the Lord's dramatic symbolism is not properly represented if the minister merely repeats the words of institution, and then hands out the bread and wine to the serving deacons. It is his duty to take bread and break it in the sight of the assembled communicants, and likewise to take the cup and present it as he speaks the words concerning it. In many Nonconformist chapels this is not now done. I suppose the practice has fallen into disuse because of a dislike of what is not very accurately called ' ritualism '; yet it would seem a curious excess of Puritanism which makes Christ's disciples look askance at the ' ritualistic ' actions of their Lord. Moreover, Holy Communion is a service of dramatic action (it cannot be otherwise while the table is spread and the bread and the wine are received), and, if this service has spiritual value, it is quite irrational to minimise the symbolism as much as possible. Our Puritan forbears, whatever their shortcomings, were not guilty of this absurdity, and in this matter the Presbyterians have preserved a sound tradition more faithfully than have some other non-episcopalian bodies.

It goes without saying that if the 'manual acts' are to be properly performed a piece of bread must be provided of sufficient size to be broken in the sight of the congregation, and there must be a cup . . . but to this latter point we will return presently.

There remains to mention the communion, and the only need here is to urge the importance of an adequate period of silence. If any part of the service is curtailed, let it not be the silence.

These references to important constituents of the service are not intended to amount to a directory for the ordering of the rite; there are plenty of such directories, and it is not my purpose to add to their number. Unless our churchmanship is deplorably provincial we should appreciate that this historic rite of the Church is one where individual caprice is least admissible. A study of the directories provided, *e.g.*, in the *Common Order* of the United Church of Canada or in the *Book of Common Order, 1928* of the Scottish Church, will show that it is possible to be in touch with the age-long tradition of the Church Catholic without being false to Protestant principles or to the genius of the Evangelical Free Churches.

v

The ceremony of the communion of the cup is a great symbolical act of Christian fellowship within the New Covenant; by the sharing of the one sacred cup the unity of the brotherhood is expressed and strengthened.

Unfortunately, early in the present century the middle classes in this country became acutely conscious of microbes, and one of the first effects of this consciousness is to make you squeamish about drinking with your neighbour out of the same vessel. You never know . . .

The recently acquired science and the even more recently acquired sensitiveness introduced a disturbing element into the Communion Service. (Hygieia is an exacting goddess, and once you have acknowledged her she will never allow you to forget her.) What was to be done? The answer was perfectly simple : let there be provided a separate cup for each communicant.

Progressive Nonconformists, happily unhampered by the restrictions of tradition or of an external authority, were quickly able to put things right, and 'individual cups' were introduced into many churches. It was a simple solution. Indeed it was so simple that it failed to take into account the obtrusive fact that 'individual cups' are the blank denial of what the ceremony of the cup is supposed to express. Not only do they express symbolically the wrong meaning, they make the proper action of the ceremony impossible. When the minister comes to the words 'After the same manner also he took the cup', it is his duty (this being a re-enactment of the Last Supper) to take the cup into his hands; but, the church being hygienic and up-to-date, he finds to his confusion that there is no cup to take, and in its place a tray of rudimentary liqueur glasses. To raise that would be dramatically ludicrous, for the action and the words spoken would be absurdly inappropriate to one another.

The solecism of individual cups is far more serious in churches which hold a Protestant view about the nature of the sacrament than it would be in churches holding a 'Catholic' view, because for the Protestant the sacrament is the whole ceremony with its symbols and its actions,

and the word is not to be applied to the conse-
crated elements alone. The Catholic speaks of
'reserving' the sacrament; for a Protestant to
do so (except when he is referring to the Catholic
theory) is to talk nonsense. You cannot
'reserve' a drama.*

It is difficult to conceive anything much less
suggestive of the one loaf than the Catholic
wafer, and Protestants object to it for that
reason; but are the Nonconformist 'individual
cups' a whit more suggestive of the one chalice?
To the Catholic this may not be of great
importance, but to the Protestant it is.

The damage is done, and it is hard to see
how it can be completely remedied. Once
entertain the thought of germs, and there is no
purgative which will entirely get rid of it. I
doubt whether those churches which have
adopted 'individual cups' could return to the
older way with any comfort of mind. On the
other hand, an awakened appreciation of the
meaning of the sacrament should make the new
usage intolerable, at least if it is unmodified.

I am puzzled to find a satisfactory solution to
this problem. We might borrow from Roman

* This constitutes no objection to the laudable practice
of extending the celebration by taking the elements to the
sick at the conclusion of the service in chapel.

practice, according to which the laity communicate only in one kind,* but that would be highly unsatisfactory for us who lay great stress on the association of the rite with the Last Supper. No, to abolish the communion of the cup is not a solution.

One thing at least seems quite evident, namely, that there must be a chalice on the communion table. Without it the symbolism is all wrong, and, moreover, the minister is unable to perform the manual acts. Perhaps the best compromise would be for the minister and serving deacons to receive from the chalice, and for the rest of the communicants to be served with separate cups. That probably is the least unfortunate solution, but it is sufficiently open to objection to make one hope that those churches which have hitherto held out against the innovation of the tray will never be tempted to capitulate.

VI

As was recalled above, the sacrament of the Lord's Supper is not to be dissociated from the

* This was a growing custom which was made into a rule of the Church early in the 15th century at the Council of Constance. Vid. G. Rietschel, *Lehrbuch der Liturgik*, Vol. I., p. 391 f.

ministry of the Word : the reading and preaching of the Word. This association is habitual and emphatic in Protestant churches, but it has obtained in the Church from very early times —centuries before the Reformation. It is true that the homily vanished from the Roman Mass at an early period,* but the elaborate ceremonial † belonging to the reading of the Gospel bears witness to the importance which was once attached to the reading of the Word. The custom in the Anglican (as also the Roman) rite is for the congregation to stand during the reading of the Gospel, and it is noteworthy that the place which the Book of Common Prayer assigns to the sermon is in the Office of Holy Communion.

Real preaching (as opposed to lecturing or to giving a talk on morals or any general topic) in the Protestant conception takes the place of the Elevation of the Host in the Mass. It is, to quote the late Dr. R. S. Simpson, ' the presenting of Christ to men and to women in *words*, and when in ordinary worship the preacher delivers his sermon . . . he is presenting before men, through the medium of symbols (that is to say,

* Vid. Duchesne, *Christian Worship : Its Origin and Evolution*, E.T., 2nd ed., p. 170 f.

† Vid. P. Maranget, *The Roman Mass*, E.T., pp. 28–30.

of words suffused with his own personality), the
Person and meaning of Jesus Christ '.*   In the
sacrament of the Lord's Supper, he continues,
'Christ, Who in ordinary worship is presented
to us through *words* in preaching, is there presented to us through *actions*, and the actions are
those of His own choosing, in which the redeem-
ing love of God to us in Him is shown and conveyed to us through the Bread and the Wine
which He puts into the communicant's hands '.†
One mode of presentation does not render the
other superfluous, but it is the same Christ who
is presented. The importance of the two is
borne witness to by the experience of the
Church. This truth is exemplified by the
words of the old Scottish preacher, Robert
Bruce, which Simpson cites, and I cannot
forbear to repeat the citation :—' It would be
speered, Quherefore are sacraments annexed,
seeing we gat na mair in the sacrament nor we
get in the word ? Thy hart cannot wist nor
imagine a greater gift nor to have the Sonne of
God, quha is King of heaven and earth. And,
therefore, I say, quhat new thing wald thou
have ? The sacrament is appointed, that we

* *Ideas in Corporate Worship*, p. 27. The author is
writing of the Scottish conception of preaching, but the
conception is common to Puritans and is by no means
exclusively Scottish.   † ibid., p. 28.

may get a better grip of Christ nor we get in the simple word. The sacraments are appointed that I might have Him mair fullie in my saul; that He might make the better residence in me. This, na doubt, is the cause quherefore thir seales are annexed to the evident of the simple word.' *

In the Free Churches the ordinance of the Lord's Supper is almost invariably observed at the close of an ordinary service, so that the sacrament and the ministry of the Word are held in close association. Where the sacrament is treasured, the whole spiritual orientation of the prior service is such as to make it quite plainly an ante-communion service, only separable from the Eucharist as the Mass of the Catechumens was separable from the Mass of the Faithful in primitive times.

There ought to be no doubt in the minds of the worshippers that the 'preaching' service is leading up to its culmination in the sacrament. Perhaps if the vital relation between the two parts were brought more obviously into prominence there would be a less crowded exodus of church members before the Communion than frequently occurs at the present day. No amount of emphasis on the connexion between

* Quoted Simpson, ibid., p. 28 f.

the two will be of avail, however, unless one condition is observed : the ante-communion service must be SHORT, and by short I do not mean a trifle curtailed, but SHORT.

Holy Communion is a service of great devotional intensity; it is to misuse a means of grace to choose a time for it when the faculties of mind and spirit are exhausted. A service may be fatiguing for two reasons : because it is uninteresting or because it has called out the energies of the worshippers in attention and in worship. Thus a living service of the Word is little better than a dead one as a preface to the sacrament if it has made sufficient demand on the worshippers to tire them. Common sense should warn us that if the Offices are to be as profitable as they should be the ante-communion plus the Communion should occupy little, if any, more time than an ordinary normal ' preaching ' service. This is an elementary psychological consideration; yet we seem slow to see it, and still slower to act on it.*

* Cf. M. Bertrand : ' Lorsque la Sainte Cène est célébrée au terme d'un culte déjà long, où l'on a fait appel largement aux facultés d'attention, de recueillement, et surtout aux capacités d'adoration des fidèles, il est douteux que ceux-ci soient encore en état de recevoir dans leur plénitude les grâces qui leur sont offertes. L'ensemble du service reli-

The Lord's Supper

VII

The prevalent practice in the Free Churches is to celebrate the Lord's Supper once a month. This fact sets in relief the difference between the Protestant and the Catholic conceptions of the sacrament. Here is not the place to argue the rights and wrongs of the two conceptions. The Protestant position is the one taken in this book, and it is enough to say that our view of the precious sacredness of the rite requires us to be on our guard lest it should be staled and made common by too frequent repetition. My Catholic friends, I am aware, will say this is further evidence of the Protestant's inability to think of worship except in terms of psychological effects. Well . . . but no, I am determined to keep clear of the controversy here.

'I do not think', says Dr. F. C. Burkitt, 'that the clergy always realize that a kind of belief in the value of Holy Communion, and in the religion which Holy Communion represents,

---

gieux qui devait être une préparation est devenu un obstacle pour un pasteur peut-être épuisé, pour une Assemblée fatiguée et plus ou moins consciemment déprimée par l'exode, pas toujours silencieux, de la grande majorité des assistants.' *L'Église*, p. 62.

is sometimes dumbly testified by staying away, more than by perfunctory attendance.' * Let the Nonconformists' infrequent celebrations be also a dumb testimony to the holiness of the most sacred rite of the Christian Church.

* *The Modern Churchman*, Vol. XXII, Nos. 5, 6, and 7, p. 306.

THE END